HARRY SHAW

LEMMY...IN HIS OWN WORDS

Copyright © 2002 Omnibus Press
(A division of Music Sales Limited)

Designed by Hilite Design
Picture research by Nikki Lloyd

ISBN: 0.7119.9109.X
Order No: OP 48697

Exclusive Distributors
Music Sales Limited,
8/9 Frith Street, London W1D 3JB, UK.

Music Sales Corporation,
257 Park Avenue South, New York, NY 10010, USA.

Macmillan Distribution Services,
53 Park West Drive, Derrimut, Vic 3030, Australia.

To the Music Trade only:
Music Sales Limited,
8/9 Frith Street, London W1D 3JB, UK.

Photo credits:
Front cover: John Dee/Rex; back cover: Eddie Boldizsar/Rex.
All other photos courtesy of London Features Int.

Every effort has been made to trace the copyright holders of
the photographs in this book but one or two were
unreachable. We would be grateful if the photographers
concerned would contact us.

The author would like to thank Chris Heatley, Dave Ling and
Nephele Headleand for their help in researching this project.

Printed in Great Britain

A catalogue record for this book is available from
the British Library.

Visit Omnibus Press on the web at
www.omnibuspress.com

OMNIBUS PRESS

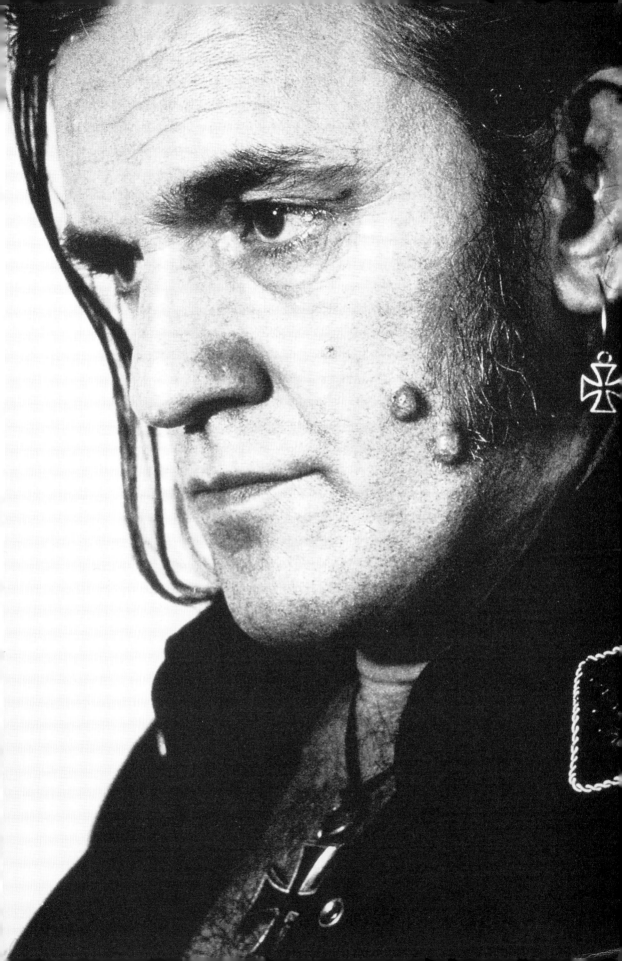

When it comes to rock'n'roll death wishes, Motörhead's 'Ace Of Spades' (with its 'I don't wanna live forever' line) ranks all the way up there with the Who's 'My Generation'. Some would say it's amazing that the man who wrote it – Ian 'Lemmy' Kilmister – has got this far, given his well-known penchant for rock'n'roll debauchery and long-term substance abuse.

But November 2000 found him celebrating his band's 25th year at London's Brixton Academy and looking good for 25 more. During that time, he and his band had transcended the heavy-metal ghetto to become all-round showbiz stars. All this, though, seemed highly unlikely when he formed the band in 1975, having been summarily sacked by Hawkwind after a drugs bust at the Canadian border. At the time, the self-styled psychedelic warlords were still surfing on the success of 'Silver Machine', which Lemmy had sung, and it was arguable if either would survive the split. Both did, and Lemmy thrived in an atmosphere where he could call the shots. The former Hendrix roadie took the name of a Hawkwind B-side he'd written as the moniker of his new outfit, and the famous black 'logo' T-shirts have since become the ultimate (and highly unlikely) fashion accessory for It Girls, rockers, punks and all points in-between. You couldn't make it up – but would they have been as keen on his first choice of name, Bastard? The original line-up of the band, a power trio, was ex-Pink Fairy Larry Wallis on guitar and Lucas Fox on drums. *New Musical Express* writer Nick Kent immediately reviewed them as "the worst band in the world", but Lemmy, as ever, couldn't have given a Flying V.

His aim, "to be like the MC5 – fast and vicious," saw the band gain converts from both punk and metal camps, plus any Hawkwinders still in earth orbit. Replacing Wallis and Fox with 'Fast' Eddie Clarke and 'Philthy Animal' Taylor respectively, he set the controls for five years of success that would climax in 1981 with the Number 1 live album *No Sleep Till Hammersmith*. For a heavy metal band to top the charts was rare, a live album unheard-of. And though the dream ticket of Kilmister/Taylor/Clarke dissolved soon afterwards, Motörhead – lining up in 2001 as Lemmy, Swedish drummer Mikkey Dee and guitarist Phil Campbell – remain the standard by which all cult bands are judged.

In truth, though, it's not the personnel but the attitude that marks Motörhead out from the rest, and will do as long as Lemmy (now a Los Angeles resident) draws breath. A 1997 London gig saw more celebs in the audience than on stage, with the likes of Primal Scream, Ben Folds Five and Elastica in attendance. Skunk Anansie guitarist Ace credits them with inspiring him to pick up a guitar, while Foo Fighter Dave Grohl labels Lemmy "the greatest rock'n'roll star of all time" – and he's known one or two.

So stand by for some inimitable and not especially politically correct comment from a man who's been there, done that and designed the T-shirt…

Growing Up

It was 1950, and for some reason there was no anaesthetic you could give to a kid that young. So what they used to do was take you to the infirmary, hold you down and rip your teeth out. (On the removal of ten teeth at the age of four.)

I had a farm in Wales with two stallions bought for £34 which I'd broke in myself. Then I heard Little Richard, sold the horses and away I went. **1991**

I was expelled from school, but I was the teacher's pet in English because I was very good at it. We had this lady teacher. I don't think it was sexual. She put me in this storeroom with the GCSE English paper when I was 13 and I passed it by 20 per cent. **1998**

My father was the most grovelling piece of scum on this earth, a weasel of a man with glasses and a bald spot. I've met him twice; the last time he said, 'What can I do to repay the damage I've done to you? I feel so guilty.' I said 'Give me a grand then just forget it - I need some new equipment.' **1999**

I was the only English kid in seven hundred Welsh. I didn't have any friends, either. **1996**

I was quite introverted until I got to my teens, always on the outside - the Watcher! But rock'n'roll don't half bring you out of yourself. **1999**

My mother was disapproving. I remember when I got my first Teddy Boy jacket. It was powder blue with a very thin red stripe, double-breasted, one button, you know. Very hot. She hated that. But everybody who ever became individualistic, in any way, has got a lot of flak from their parents. Because it isn't like what they did themselves and they hate that. It means you've left the nest. **1999**

I worked in a factory in Colwyn Bay. They told me to get my hair cut or get a hair net - said it was a hazard! **1978**

I was one of the first people to have one of them studded leather jackets and be in a band you know. I've still got me a sartorial cut-offs and me bullet belt as well. I lived with the Angels in London between '75 and '77: we had this big house in Chelsea that we shared with some guys from the England chapter. **1979**

From top: Little Richard, Elvis, Bill Haley, The Who and Chuck Berry.

Heroes and Influences

Little Richard - 'Lucille' and 'Good Golly Miss Molly'. That's what got me. **1996**

Elvis was the first. I mean, Bill Haley came out before him but I didn't really believe in him because he was fat and had this silly kiss-curl on his head. Elvis didn't smile, he sneered and he had sideburns. He was skinny and he was bad news. We wanted some loud, there wasn't any loud, then; you don't understand what it was like before rock'n'roll! I mean, before loud we were getting Frank Sinatra, Lita Roza, Ronnie Carroll and Dickie Valentine. **1994**

Chuck Berry was the first one to write smart lyrics, the first one to really tell a story in a song, about driving out in your car and going up the hill for a bit of slap and tickle. At the time we didn't realise Chuck was black, because there were no pictures of anybody then. You just got these amazing releases from America in a little paper sleeve, but didn't know anything about them. Chuck Berry was really on the pulse for a long time. **1994**

Little Richard was the ultimate in defiance. I loved him because he was nuts. He is still my favourite of all. He lives in the Hyatt on Sunset Boulevard but I've never met him and I've always wanted to. In those days, there were bigger personalities because 1) there

weren't as many of them and 2) it was the first time ever, so there were no rules. **1994**

The Who were a complete fucking cataclysm; they came on-stage, sang incredibly high, three-part harmonies and then they smashed up all of their equipment. 'Anyway, Anyhow, Anywhere' was the first thing we heard with feedback. The Beatles tried a little buzz of it at the beginning of 'I Feel Fine', but The Who were the first ones to use it as an instrument. And, of course, The Who were the first ones with Marshalls. **1994**

Once I saw Hendrix, that was it. He could do all that wild stuff and play like nobody else as well. Hendrix was so slinky with it, so graceful, he was amazing. I was really lucky to get a job with him, just a humper.

I've very few memories of Hendrix. There was a lot of acid about. It's a bit difficult trying to remember things when there are dragons coming out of the wall at you. We did get the best acid going. He came over here and Owsley was a real Hendrix groupie, so he hurried round to Hendrix's hotel and gave him a hundred thousand tabs. It wasn't even illegal then. Hendrix brought them back in his suitcase. And he just handed them round to the crew. I was with him for eight or nine months, just lifting and dragging, nothing that required talent. Was I surprised when he died? I was pissed off, I was going to audition for him that day. **2000**

You can like anything. There's all that music out there. Listen to it all and make up your own mind, no matter what your friends fuckin' think. **1996**

I like the Everly Brothers, Abba, MC5, any fuckin' thing. As long as you like it. Hell, it doesn't even have to be good, as long you like it. People can be so fuckin' stupid, they have to be told what to like. They can't exercise that much control in their own brain. Bad news, innit? **1996**

Metallica - Excellent, unstoppable. **1996**

I like the old blues like Little Walter, Junior Parker, Memphis Slim… Any of those guys I like. **1999**

The Ramones understood rock'n'roll. You hear the chord progressions and the solos, they must have been great rock'n'roll fans when they were kids. I heard myself in them, and they heard themselves in me. I think everything you hear influences you, either for or against it. The Yardbirds were a big influence on me, you know. They made me want to play like them. **2000**

From top: The Yardbirds, Metallica and The Ramones.

Surviving The Sixties

I was with The Rainmakers and The Motown Sect in Manchester, playing all this awful soul shit in order to survive. Still, those records like 'Leaving Here' and 'No Good Without You Baby' are among my favourites. It was a great period musically… but I was getting nowhere with that band. **1981**

We used to do 'Smokestack Lightning' and 'Baby What's Wrong' by The Downliners Sect. The scene was all Motown, so we figured if we called ourselves The Motown Sect we'd get gigs. We got a year's worth out of that. **1991**

The Rockin' Vicars were the first pop ground to play behind the Iron Curtain: We got the Yugoslav Youth Orchestra or something; they got The Rockin' Vicars. **1978**

One night I was in the Oasis in Manchester and The Rockin' Vicars were on. They all had hair down to their arses and I thought that was wonderful because everybody else was wearing the Mod jackets, the shoes and doing that studied Mod walk and everything, and I really didn't fit in! I had the hair and an old combat jacket and I didn't give a fuck. Anyway, the Vicars were getting mobbed up there, they were never much on record but those were the days up there for them, you could pick up a pile of phone numbers off your truck after a gig, all written in lipstick, so I

thought 'this looks like fun' and I heard from one of their roadies that their guitar player was leaving, he said he'd let me know.

A few weeks later I'm back in Wales and I get this phone call: "Can you play lead?" I said yeah but I didn't have any bloody idea at all. I got an audition at their flat in Salford and somehow managed to blag them that I could play lead. They had a gig that night and they used to do this Who thing at the end of it, smashing up all the gear, everything. I loved this, didn't I? I'd been given a guitar, this stack of gear, it wasn't even my equipment. So I went raving mad, stuck the guitar through the speakers, ran around with the guitar whining and screaming, plugged the other guitar in, smashed it against the first one, up on the piano at the side of the stage, they thought I was the cat's pyjamas! I couldn't play lead very well, but it was a great act. **1981**

When I was with The Rockin' Vicars, we had a routine where I would throw a pie in the bass player's face. One night we didn't have a pie, there was only a metal pie plate, but they ordered me to do the show anyway. So I chucked the plate in his face… broke the poor bleeder's nose in three places! **May 1980**

The Rockin' Vickers only used to play up in the North. We were huge.

13

We could sell out the Bolton Locarno by ourselves. We wore dog collars and the Finish national costume, the Lapp smock, royal blue with orange and yellow felt stick-on stuff across - and skin-tight white jeans with lace-up flies, and reindeer skin boots. Seemed like a good idea at the time. Believe me, we made a lot of bread. We paid no tax, making £200 a week clear. I had two Jags and a Chevy, we had a speedboat on fucking Windermere. We were a class act; we had the first double bass-drums in England. And they still play on the cabaret circuit. **1991**

The Rockin' Vicars lasted two years, or maybe a bit less. From '66 to middle '67. Then I went to London and got into Opal Butterfly and Sam Gopal. Sam Gopal first, actually. Neither of them was much of a thing. When I joined Opal Butterfly they were already on the way out. **1996**

Jimi Hendrix

I was going along to gigs and the next thing I was humping on the (Hendrix) tour for a tenner a week. It was Hendrix, The Move, Pink Floyd with Syd Barrett, Amen Corner, The Nice with Davy O'List, and Eire Apparent who became The Grease Band. All for 7/6. It was great fun seeing Hendrix at the height of his power, after that he only did *Electric Landlady* (sic) and then he was gone. I was at all the sessions for *Axis: Bold As Love*, and once at the management offices I remember Hendrix coming in backwards with a typewriter in his fucking hands going. 'Yeah, I'm the backwards man, yeah!' and going out backwards though the other door. When he was playing I'd watch him on stage from a chair in the wings; you could never tell how he did it. He loved to fuck off all the guitar players in the audience. Graham Nash used to sit backstage with his ear on the stacks all night, none of this glad-handing you get backstage now with the fucking canapés; in those days people wanted to learn and improve. **1991**

When I came down to London in 1967, after leaving the Vicars, I went to stay at Ron Wood's mum's house. Then I got the gig with Hendrix, just humping gear and scoring acid for him. It was like The Rocking Vicars to the power of 12. I mean, it was fucking madness. **1999**

Jimi would send me out to score 10 acid trips. He'd take six, and I'd keep four. **2000**

Hawkwind in 1973, left to right:
Nik Turner, Del Deltmar, Dik Mik, Simon King,
Lemmy and Dave Brock.

The Hawkwind Years

When I was in Hawkwind we had to go cap in hand to our manager for every pound we got. That's how the 'Lemmy a quid 'til Friday' thing came about. It's been following me ever since. **1981**

I was sick of dealing dope. I was looking to join a band, and I was also taking more and more speed: I was up and out of it all the time. Dik Mik suddenly arrives out of his mind at my squat in the middle of the night. We started taking and soon realised we were both interested in how long you could make the human body jump about without stopping. We did that for a few months till he ran out of money and wanted to rejoin Hawkwind. But he wanted to take his new friend with him. "What do you want to do?" they said. "Lead guitarist will do," I said. Their old guitarist, Huw Lloyd Langton, had taken some acid at the Isle of Wight Festival and said, "I'm going for a walk, boys," and that was the last they saw of him for five years! **1991**

Our show has never really been worked out... it's an absolute mess - but it works. If we did it any other way, we'd turn into Yes or ELP. **1973**

I'm just an old rocker with his hair grown long, but Hawkwind fits exactly into my philosophy. They're weird - that suits me. **1973**

We used to go on stage in all kinds of messes, and we spiked all the food and drink down the Roundhouse with acid. We were very irresponsible. Dik Mik played a ring modulator fixed up to a fuzzbox and a wah-wah pedal set up on a card-table. It goes out of the range of human hearing at both ends, and we used to be able to get the epileptics in the audience. We used to lock the doors to keep people in and fire strobes at them at eye-level, it wasn't the fast ones that fucked you up, it was the slow ones. The first time I ever saw Hawkwind was at the Roundhouse; they went chug-chug for an hour and the audience were stuck in the same pose for the whole time. I thought fuck me, I've got to join them; I certainly can't watch them! **1991**

When Hawkwind played Wembley Stadium, Robert Calvert came on-stage in a witches hat with a trumpet and sword. After the second song he attacked me with the sword, so I belted him around the head with my bass and he went away and tortured someone else. **1999**

Dave Brock and Nik Turner were always brained. Nick came out on-stage one night in Harlow dressed as a frog. It was raining like hell and there was all these freaks sitting around with tarpaulin over them. We started playing and Nick came out with these green tights and a green leotard. He fell off the stage and into this big pond! I had to go offstage, I was literally on my knees laughing. **1999**

They'd tried everybody else in the band to sing 'Silver Machine' and there was only me and the drummer left. And I sang it very, very well first time and the others all fucking hated it. then it went to No. 1 in the *New Musical Express* chart and they really hated it! **2000**

We were living in the van together. We'd fuck the same chick together. It was very together until certain people in the band started being élitist. The rest of us were becoming a draaag, bad vibes, man. The cosmicity was leaving the band and it's all your fault. We became polarised, a shame because when things were right we'd come to your town and fuck your head up! Anyway, we were on tour in America, going to Detroit, then Canada. We stopped in Niles, Michigan, but I didn't want to eat because I was a speed-freak, so I went out with my new Spotmatic camera. But I got smacked over the head and got my camera nicked, I never even saw the assailant. I got up and went back to the roadhouse and they'd fucked off without me! So with only 20 bucks I had to hitchhike across Michigan, homosexual truckers, VW Microbuses full of fucking bozo hippies - and finally got in at seven in the morning.
I checked in, slept for four hours, did the soundcheck and gig, slept, got up again three hours later, got in the car, forgot to put my speed away, went through the border, where I was searched and busted. I was on a chain-gang in Cook County jail for 10 days and was ready for the louse-powder with my overalls over my arm when the most wonderful voice I've ever heard said behind me, "Kilmister, you're bailed." I was put on a plane to Toronto, everybody said happy to see you again, did the show, and four o'clock that morning was fired because they thought there might be future legal problems touring America. And their publicity said they were the most cosmic band on the planet. **1991**

I can't really complain because if I hadn't been fired from Hawkwind, I would never have got Motörhead together. But it did hurt, yeah. **1999**

I loved being in the band. It's not the case that they're bastards who I'll never speak to again, I mean when you're on stage with somebody, whatever happens off stage doesn't matter. That thing will always be like that, because you don't talk to them on stage, you play with them. You can hate somebody when you're on stage but you still play with them. That even kept The Who together. Me and Dave Brock and Simon King were a great fucking three-piece band. **1989**

Actually, I really do like Bob Calvert because he's like an absolute maniac – and I do like a good maniac! **1977**

Being fired from Hawkwind for drugs is a bit like being pushed off the Empire State Building for liking heights, you know? I was doing the wrong drugs. I was doing speed and they were all acid freaks. Mind you, I was doing acid as well, it was just one of those elitist numbers, Nik Turner actually apologised to me six months ago. It took him 25 years, but he finally apologised to me. I said, 'Thanks Nik, that's really helped a lot'. **2000**

The only reason they bailed me out of jail, apparently, was because my replacement couldn't get there on time. It's a terrible thing to be fired? Especially for an offence that everyone else was guilty of. So I came home and fucked all their old ladies. Not the ugly ones, of course. But at least four. I took great pleasure in it. Eat that, you bastards! **2000**

I was told I was being sacked. I said 'Thanks very much' and left the room. I must tell you I was upset. Tears were seen. Anyway, I pleaded not guilty and the charges were dismissed. They must have wanted me out. I was afterwards told that Nik Turner had said that if I rejoined he'd leave; dunno whether it's true or not. But afterwards Dave Brock phoned me up, invited me back. I liked that. I wanna put that on the record. It was the only nice thing that happened. In fact, they'd already flown Paul Rudolph (ex-Pink Fairies) out to Canada to take my place - and they hadn't even told me! **1975**

I gave it a kick. And then they replaced me with the worst possible choice, fuckin' Paul Rudolph. He was a jazz-slanted player. Fuckin' hopeless. **1996**

They were the sort of band that flashes and dies, and them flashes and dies again. They were unique. For me, they were better than the Floyd. They were getting into more interesting places, given the Floyd's success. Because the Floyd just lapsed into this fucking pop music with lights. **1999**

One thing about Hawkwind, you either loved us or you hated us. There wasn't any of that 'They're okay' stuff. You either became a trusted, loyal, devoted follower or you fucking couldn't stand it and ran howling from the room. **1999**

We attracted every fucking headcase going! **2000**

The 1972/73 Hawkwind in line-up, left to right: Simon King, Dik Mik, Lemmy, Dave Brock, Bob Calvert, Nik Turner and Del Deltmar.

The Motörhead band of 1975-82, left to right: 'Philthy' Phil Taylor, Lemmy and 'Fast' Eddie Clarke.

Motörhead: The Band

Well, I got me a new band. Motörhead. Meet Lucas Fox, drums. Then there's Larry Wallis, ex-Pink Fairies. I'm still looking for another guitar player. Someone foxy. It's gonna be a... uh... a great band. **1975**

If we move next door to you, your lawn will die. **1975**

What people don't realise is that all the money goes back into the show, there's no money going around in Motörhead. I've got a really good overdraft, my bank manager hates me. **1982**

Now it's my band I'm as happy as a pig in shit. **1982**

We've been going four years longer that the Third Reich. **1991**

Motörhead is American slag for speed freak. I originally wanted to get a band like the MC5 together. In fact, it ended up not sounding anything like the MC5. **1978**

We're very good musicians really. I auditioned for the part of Joni Mitchell but I failed the physical. As long as the kids like us that's all I play for. I don't play for no critics. **1980**

Motörhead is a universal thing. It goes for everybody. We don't segregate our audience. Anybody who watches our thing and enjoys it deserves a place to see us. **1980**

We've been skint for years, haven't we Phil? What have you got in your bank account? I know what I've got - £200 overdraft! **1982**

Fame and fortune? I'll be famous, but I'll never be rich. If I had a million dollars a day I'd spend it all on goodies. **1978**

I was the only one with a pedigree behind me. Not that it was worth much, a worm-eaten pedigree. But it worked as far as the press were concerned, we were called Lemmy's Motörhead for the first six months. **1991**

I just had a very clear vision of what I wanted to play and the only way I could do it was to form the band that I did. I wanted it to be like the MC5 - fast and vicious, yeah. I didn't want to be the singer, though. I was just gonna be the bass player. I wanted to get a singer in, but of course we couldn't find one. And it was cheaper, because I was already there. **1999**

MC5 were just an excellent rock'n'roll band. That first live album never got anywhere, never did any business for them and, to a large extent, Motörhead followed in their footsteps. We've always been a cult sort of band without making it big, except for one big flash before being relegated to cult status again. **1994**

Motörhead: Records you can ride a bike across without scratching it. **1980**

I hate rehearsing, if I can get out of it in any way, I'll do it. **1991**

There is no plan to this band. We've never had one. That's why we've lasted so long. Plans run you off you feet. I believe in spontaneity, which we certainly have. **1998**

It's not like we were trying to specifically be the 'loudest band in the world'. We just like it loud. The thing is with being loud, you've got to be fairly good or else it'll just be a mess, although one man's impenetrable mess is another man's pure music. **2000**

At Port Vale, we built the entire stage out of PAs. A guy called up from four miles away while we were soundchecking and said he couldn't hear his TV. **2000**

My earliest recollections of Motörhead involve incredible poverty, living in squats. This bird we knew called Aeroplane Gaye used to work under a furniture store in Chelsea, and if anyone quit early we'd all dash down there and rehearse. We were that broke, but we did all right. We were struggling for a long time with no bread, then over about six months it just went whammo. **2000**

Was I always convinced of the band's value? Well, maybe not during that little era with Lucas, but after we got Eddie and Phil in I knew we had something special. That was an excellent band from day one. I'd only written three songs for Hawkwind and I wasn't too good at it yet. But this band has always been the eternal underdog, and we're good at it. **2000**

I don't remember exactly which one of us said to call it Motörhead, but I was the one who had to agree to it, so therefore it was my idea. **2000**

Phil is definitely playing great. Mikkey is a monster. **1996**

Oh, sure, I am Motörhead and Motörhead is me, but this is a very democratic band and every member has his say. **1984**

Motörhead T-shirts - it's just a thing in Top Shop, innit? I don't thing it's in the interest of Motörhead, it's just in the interests of quirky fashion. Meg Mathews and Mel C should come to a show, you know? They'd find out what fucking quirky can mean. Or come backstage and talk to Phil Campbell - that's quirky! **2000**

I was first in America in '75, but this is much better. We were headlining, Hawkwind, but I don't think the reception we got was a good at this. It's amazing, kids are shouting for numbers off Overkill which is unreleased here. There are die-hards in every town and there's not been a single beer can thrown, yet I've seen opening bands die such horrible deaths over here. **1982**

We'll go on and survive because we're rebels. We're the bad guys and people always find the bad guys are more interesting, especially with everything becoming more sterile. I think Motörhead have become the backbone of British music. We mean something worldwide. **1984**

Listen, we've had that 'This is your year, boys' crap every year of our career. It's never been our fucking year, all they give you is excuses like 'I've hurt my back' or 'The man didn't have the right form'. I'm waiting for the year when they don't say anything, then we should do well. **1992**

I think we are perceived of being from before, and that people would rather have bands of their own age group. That's fair enough because when I was a kid I wanted the Stones and The Beatles. We were too late for every craze; we were too early for heavy metal and too late for the New Wave of British Heavy Metal. We couldn't get signed while all that was going on and then when we did we were like runners-up. We're a very difficult band to market; we rely on word of mouth. But we're making good records, and as long as we can keep doing that then that's all I care about. **1992**

I always figured that if the band is working as far as the band is concerned then fuck the rest of it. I never thought I was gonna make a living, 'cos you never do. It's just a band and you've been in and out of

bands for years. Just another adventure, but it turned out all right. I never thought this is how I'll play the bass and I never thought I'll go and live there or I'll get a band together in this format. I never thought I'd have two guitarists on purpose. I never thought I'll make it a three piece on purpose, I always followed an impulse.'

I think Motörhead is one of those bands that'll be appreciated when it's gone. I think we'll be like The Yardbirds were after they were gone. Nobody gave a fuck about them when they were here, they went down in a flurry of disinterest. **1989**

No one has fun all the time, and we didn't get here by imperial grant, we got it by working for it. Würzel's got his life of Riley now simply by living through a load of shit for years, and then writing me a letter saying 'I hear you want an unknown guitarist, and there's nobody more unknown that me.' So I thought, this man shows an adequate grasp of the ridiculous, and signed him up immediately! His guitar playing was brilliant, and I fancied him because he had a sense of humour, and that's what you need. He's like me, he does it for the pure joy of it. **1985**

We're really proud of Motörhead, we're still a valid band and we're doing things on there that (ex-guitarist) Fast Eddie Clarke and (former drummer) 'Philthy Animal' Taylor couldn't do. We're playing the best music we've ever made. **2000**

*Motörhead, circa 1987, left to ri[c]
Lemmy, Phil Taylor, Phil Campbell and Wur.*

Hellos and Goodbyes

Larry (Wallis) worries. As soon as he gets hold of anything, he drops it on his toe. Brian Robertson's another one. He is a fucking marvellous musician, but he cannot work with people. Like Larry. It's just insecurity. **1991**

We fired Lucas 'cos he was trying to keep up with my habit. He was doing all this speed and the veins were standing out on his head and he was going off on his own and standing against the wall looking intense and telling me things, so I had to let him go. **1977**

Eddie was just going through one of his crazes, he used to have 'em all the time. He had this craze on this guy Will Reid-Dick, who had co-produced the Iron First album with him, and he came over to New York to do that collaboration ('Stand By Your Man', with Plasmatics singer Wendy O Williams).
Wendy, rest in peace, wasn't the type of chick who got the song right away, she had to work at it. They (Clarke and Reid-Dick) got impatient and became very counter-productive, so I ended up producing it myself while they were outside the studio bitching. To leave a band after seven years just because of that was ludicrous. He'd left several times before, but Phil and I just couldn't talk him back that time. Eddie was stupid that day. **2000**

I think Brian (Robertson)'s gonna change Motörhead, but on certain numbers he'll have to thrash, which he's quite capable of doing. He's a good wee thrasher! The back end will be the same, but the icing on the cake will be different. **1982**

We all thought that *Another Perfect Day* was one of the best albums we have ever realised. Motörhead is, however, essentially a live band and unfortunately the *Perfect Day* material did not come over on stage as powerfully as on the album. We've decided we've given it our best shot, and it hasn't worked out. But we'll be back with a roar in '84, be there or cut your hair. **1983**

Brian did America and Japan with us and that was great. But on an English tour he started going silly. He destroyed the feeling for the band. He's a wonderful guitar player and a great writer, but he couldn't crack it on stage and he wouldn't do the old songs. He destroyed people's feeling for the band. On stage he repelled a lot of the old fans and never won any new ones for us. The fan club went down from 6,000 to less than 100 at one point. It was just miserable, y'know. He's his own worst enemy. Sacked? He was pushed – actually, he was almost catapulted. **1989**

I said to Robbo, I hope we can be better friends now than when we were working together, because I was better friends with him before he joined us. He's a brilliant guitarist and he could reproduce everything he played on that album live, but a lot of the time he didn't. He was playing like a killer before the album and everywhere we went – America, Japan and Europe – people were falling over in amazement. But of course when we get back home he falls to bits. I'm sure he felt threatened by me on-stage because I'm not yer average bass player. I'm always out front and he couldn't handle it. Our loyal fans never accepted him because he didn't work hard enough on-stage to try to win them over. If he wasn't getting a reaction, he'd just stand there and accept it. He didn't try to be 'in' the band, he was always Brian Robertson with Motörhead – and even though he's a much better guitarist than Eddie Clarke, he didn't fit in as well. I want to go one step backwards so we can go two steps forward. I want a guitarist who is a bit more in tune with Motörhead. I want somebody who can upstage me – someone who can make me work hard night after night. Robbo let me do all the work because he believed the people had come to see me and me only so he didn't try too hard. I want someone who is going to stand toe to toe and trade it with me. When we do get him we'll do an album, probably got to America and Europe and then come back to England, playing shit hot and kick everyone in the teeth who thinks we're dead. They can

ignore us for a little while, but not for long – because we're gonna come back and saw their heads off!
1983

When Phil (Taylor) left it was like a part of my family was gone. For an hour or two afterwards I wondered whether I just shouldn't jack it all in.
1984

The way Eddie left wasn't all right, but the way Phil left was amicable. He just called myself and Doug Smith, our manager, in one day and said he'd run his course with Motörhead. I've got a lot

of respect for Phil. I wish him lots of luck in whatever he does. It's just one of those things. After nine years I know the geezer closer than a brother. If he says he wants to leave, he's obviously done a lot of thinking about it. I know Phil well enough to know that he's really considered it carefully and he's off. There's no point in going through all these numbers, "Oh please Phil don't do it" I just shook his hand, gave him a footballer's kiss and off he went. No, really; what can you do? **1984**

Brian Robertson, centre, joined Phil Taylor and Lemmy in Motörhead in 1982.

In the end, I started to put another band together. When Würzel sent in his letter he enclosed two photos taken in a Woolworth's photo booth. He was so nervous at the auditions we had to sit him in a chair and calm him down. **1984**

That's all I need at my age – to be in a band with the Bash Street Kids! On the arrival of Phil Campbell and Würzel, **1984**

I'm the basic core of Motörhead. As long as I'm in it it'll be all right. We've never had that many line-up changes, we haven't! Pete Gill was a bit of a prima donna, but he was a good drummer. I've nothing to say against Pete Gill. Pete left, he was not pushed. Thing is, people think he was pushed. They do, don't they? I hope they don't, because he wasn't. I don't know what he wants, but he's a wonderful drummer, one of the best drummers I've worked with in my life, and believe me, I've worked with plenty. Peter Gill was one of the best. Please put that in, because he deserves it. **1989**

I didn't like having to tell people we couldn't do 'Overkill' anymore because he couldn't play it, because he really should have been able to. He wasn't that old, just too out of it and apathetic, taking the wages. We warned him twice over a period of about 18 months, but he didn't buck up. He lost it, didn't care any more. You can't make people care. **On Phil Taylor's second spell, 2000**

The Young Ones was the night Phil told us he was out, well he'd told us he was out a couple of weeks beforehand, but we asked him to do *The Young Ones* with us, he said he'd do that, but that was it. He was out. **1989**

It's like losing a brother. It's a bit of a shock, especially for me since I've been with him for 17 years. Phil Taylor leaves again, **1992**

Phil was never as good when he came back. He was great before he left. He had to come back because his band that was going to be so much better than Motörhead failed miserably. So I gave him his gig back and I don't think he ever forgave me for giving it to him. He's a strange bird. He got worse, not better. When he first got back, he wasn't that bad then he went... well, by the end, it was like "What the fuck was that?" His excuse was, "Oh, I was improvising." **1995**

When Eddie left, we'd been going round and round in circles, arguing forever about the same things. Then he walked out - we were in New York - and if we'd been bothered to sit up all night trying to talk him round he would probably have stayed. But we'd been through it all so many times by then I just couldn't be bothered anymore. None of us could. Even if we had talked him back, he would just have left again later.
With Phil, it was more him wanting to go off with Brian Robertson and do something with him. Then he

came back, then he left again. That's no good. Either you're into it 100 per cent or you might as well throw the fucking towel in. **1999**

I've wanted to go for a while, but I had to pick my moment and my album, and 'Sacrifice' is a really fucking good one to go out on. Würzel, **1995**

Würzel started listening to other voices, what can I tell you? I don't know, you'd have to ask him really. He just upped and split. Well, he was getting worse. At the end he was hardly playing. He only did two solos on the last album. Before, him and Phil would have been fighting for each solo. I get to do more interesting shit. But there again, he could have done whatever he wanted in this band but he chose not to so he's playing with Crusher Joule out of the *Kerrang* paper now. It's some electronic bullshit. **1996**

We broke up in a very acrimonious way and I'll find it very had to forgive him, which is a shame because Würzel had been my best friend in the band for years. He said such terrible things about me. He accused me of stealing his money, which was disgusting. **2000**

Mikkey Dee, in a way, saved us, because he is the best drummer that we've ever had. He's excellent. **1995**

Punk & Disorderly
Motörhead & The New Wave

We've got more in common with The Damned than Judas Priest. More Sex Pistols than Black Sabbath. **1995**

Punks couldn't tell the difference if they shut their eyes. At Captain Sensible's birthday party at the Roundhouse with The Damned, The Adverts and us, I've never seen so much gobbing in my life. They were skating around in this green slime. I always thought that was quite horrible. **1991**

I don't know where Johnny Rotten's at, at the moment with all the PIL stuff. I just don't think it's what he should be doing. I think that us and The Damned are the only punk bands left. **1979**

We're a lot faster than anyone else too. That's why the punks like us. **1979**

Sid Vicious used to crash round our squat with one of the Slits. And I was making up a rhythm section with the band's drummer, Palmolive. We were all broke as shit. We'd pick up the thrown-away vegetables down the Portobello Road, cut the bad bits off and make soup. And there was a chick who could go into a shop in a pair of hot pants and a skin-tight blouse and lift a packet of cornflakes, I never knew how she did it. **1991**

In Hungary they really went for it too, chicks sitting on guys' shoulders just like the old days; none of this spitting and throwing rocks and bits of chairs. That's worrying the way that's come in. And they're not just doing it to the bands, but to themselves. The first headbanger was not just shaking his head, but smashing it on stage until his face was a mask of blood. We thought he was just an eccentric, but it turns out he was the forerunner of a new wave. Very weird. If that's what kids feel they have to do to be included in their peers, what's next? **1991**

He was all right, Sid. He was always a gentleman with me. I got quite upset when he died. He never had a chance. He was trying to be all the people he admired and it was impossible for him. But that fucking Nancy Spungen: I'd have strangled her if he hadn't have knifed her. She was the Courtney Love of her day. **2000**

Some of our first gigs were supporting The Damned which started a cross-over thing, but even so I'd say we had as big a hand in the punk thing as anyone. **1983** and me. We're very similar. We don't basically like the broad mass of you guys. Ha ha ha. We like individuals, that's about it. Scornful is the word that describes us, probably. **2000**

People ask us, are you punk or what? That's bullshit. I don't care what colour your hair is, what clothes you wear. If you dig the music, that's what it's all about. **1978**

Left, Sid and Nancy; right: Johnny Rotten

The Competition

There's more life in a frozen chicken from Tesco's than there is in Pat Travers. **1981**

Slayer weren't very good on that tour, either. But you see, I don't mind. I say good luck to them. It's not bad luck for me. I'd liked to have been more successful, but there you go, it didn't happen. It's just one of those things. It's life. **1996**

The most successful comeback thing was Kiss, wasn't it? But they're not Kiss like they were, you know? I mean, they might be better or worse, but they're not the same. You don't get the same vibe. **1999**

I almost went for a job with The Damned once. I did a gig with them. I played bass on their first show after they reformed. They got another bassist after that. It was such fun breaking everything to bits like I used to... smashing up equipment and falling on the floor, you know it's great fun. Then again I'm better off staying where I am. I have control. **1996**

Elves and dragons and all that bollocks! Ronnie James Dio does what he does and he does it very well, so why not? I just don't do that. I never saw any fairies at the bottom of my fuckin' garden, they were all out front at the pub. **1996**

The Ramones are excellent. Black day for rock'n'roll when they split up. **1996**

I think most of the Futurist thing is abominable. It seems to consist of three blokes on keyboards and somebody telling you what a drag it is in a gabardine mac! **1982**

Slipknot are nothing to do with rock'n'roll. They're not a rock band, they've got no tunes, no chords or choruses. They have no idea how to behave on stage and they wear masks and red boiler suits, I just don't see any redeeming features, well maybe one - they're pretty good at disguises. I came from The Beatles and Little Richard, they come from the circus. Maybe I'm too old to get it, but I don't mind because they're crap. **2000**

Limp Bizkit? I could make a nice bracelet out of them, or a nice pair of earrings. They're just fucking pap, garbage. Sorry. We did the Ozzfest a couple of years ago, and I went out and had a look at them the first night, and they had a giant toilet on stage, into which they were throwing pictures of The Spice Girls. I thought, "Wow, this is really cutting-edge shit! Can't wait to see some more of that!" **2000**

Imitation is the sincerest for of flattery isn't is? People getting influenced by us, I'm very pleased, obviously. It just seems a shame to me that if they're gonna be big then why can't they write their own fucking songs? It's like this rap thing, it's got to the stage now where every song you hear is pinched, with drum loops stuck on it. **1999**

Marilyn Manson has a real talent for dressing up, but then again so have most of the Royal Shakespeare Company. Skunk Anansie are the best band out of England in at least ten years. I also like a band from Berlin called Skew Siskin, and Gluecifer from Norway, and Nashville Pussy. **2000**

Clockwise, from top left: Limp Bizkit, Kiss, Skunk Anansie and Slipknot.

The Music

On Parole (1975, re-released too often to mention)

That's Ted Carroll, that is. He's always releasing things. He's a great geezer and if it wasn't for Ted there wouldn't be any Motörhead anyway, so Ted has carte blanche, he can do what he wants with the old catalogue. He's only got the old Chiswick stuff anyway. **1989**

'My least favourite Motörhead album is probably *On Parole* or *Iron Fist*. **1995**

Overkill (1979)

This was the first album on a decent label. It was a great album and the start of our chart successes, so it's always going to have a warm, cuddly place in my heart. 'Overkill' the song, sounds amazingly slow now when you listen to it on that album. **1998**

You can't ditch 'Overkill', 'Bomber', 'Iron Fist' or 'Ace Of Spades'. It wouldn't be right. If I go to see Little Richard I expect to hear 'Good Golly Miss Molly' or I'm gonna be pissed off. But I don't mind if he does a few new songs, too. I just wish people would extend me the same courtesy. Classic Rock **2000**

'I Won't Pay Your Price' (from Overkill)

I amuse the shit out of myself sometimes. When I was writing 'I Won't Pay Your Price', I fell off my chair laughing. 'Don't stop

me/don't even try/gonna stick my finger in your eye'. It was fuckin' hilarious. **1996**

Bomber (1979)

A couple of weeks ago, I was listening to 'Bomber', trying to remember the ending on it. I do listen to 'em now and again cos I think we make good records. I'll listen to them any time, even in the bath, on the beach or in bed, dressed or not. **1996**

'Ace Of Spades' (1980)

'All the best moments on our records were accidents. I never thought of 'Ace Of Spades' as anything special, it was just new. I was looking for a theme. I'd been playing the fruit machines and thought of gambling, and just wrote the song. It all fitted together, but I never thought it was a particularly brilliant song. I still don't. Wurzel says it's the complete good heavy metal song. He loves it. **1989**

'Ace of Spades' is just a catch phrase. I thought it was a really good idea when I wrote the bloody thing and it's backfired on me ever since [laughs]. I always thought it was a joke because of the tap dancing bit in the middle. Me and Phil always used to tap dance to that in the studio. **1996**

I'm sick of that song ('Ace Of Spades'). We play it first just to get it out of the way. I mean, let's face

it, there is plenty of tracks to choose from. There's 18 bloody albums out there. If you have to play 'Ace Of Spades' all the time, that's killing us, killing us dead. We've got no chance of ever progressing beyond that point if that's all they'll ever play. **1996**

'Please Don't Touch' (1981)
That single, 'Please Don't Touch' off the *St. Valentines Day Massacre* EP with Girlschool made it to Number 5. That was higher than we had done with our individual records. **1996**

No Sleep Til Hammersmith (1981)
This was our downfall, really, because how do you follow a Number 1 live album? We were fucked, immediately. On top of which we submitted a very substandard follow-up in *Iron Fist*. **1998**

The whole of that period was a blur because we were at the height of our success and our excesses. I'm not sure I really remember very much from that time so it's a good job that someone actually recorded it all. We didn't know what was going on but we knew we were on a roll. The gigs were total chaos. **2001**

We knew that *No Sleep...* was gonna do well because people had been waiting for a live album from us for three years, but never in our wildest dreams did we think it would go straight in at No 1. Actually, I was more pleased when *Ace Of Spades* went in at No. 4, because *No Sleep...* was a one-off. That said, it was also our death-knell because you can never follow a live album that goes straight in at No. 1. What are you gonna do, put out another one? **2000**

Iron Fist (1982)

Iron Fist was the worst we ever made. We produced it ourselves and that was complete self-indulgence. It was a mistake and why it was so bad. It's got mistake right through it like a stick of rock. **1989**

The album was bad, inferior to anything else we've ever done. There are at least three songs on there that were completely unfinished. Having Eddie [Clarke] produce it was a mistake that even he would now probably admit to. But there you go, we were arrogant. When you're successful that's what you become, you think it'll go on forever. **2000**

'Stand By Your Man' (1982)

I feel we've stayed pretty close to Tammy Wynette's original version, just speeded it up a fraction! **1983**

Another Perfect Day (1983)

I always liked that album, but people deserted us in their droves. It was Brian. He insisted on being a special guest instead of being in the band. It was just fucking hopeless. **1998**

Orgasmatron (1986)

We do all our albums real quick. We actually had time to write all the songs before we got into the studio. Fucking *Orgasmatron* we did in 10 days. **1995**

Rock'n'Roll (1987)

What we tend to do is to write all the tracks, then I come in with the lyrics as the last minute. Then we pick a track to call it after. *Rock'n'Roll* wasn't the best track on the album by a long shot. I wanted to call it *Blackheart* but we weren't going to do that track on stage because of all the vocals on it, so that was it out. I mean, we nearly called *Another Perfect Day Shine*, just called it after one track, or *I Got Mine*, that was another possibility for that one. Anyway we argued about this for fucking ages, about three weeks. Finally we sat round the office, the four of us plus Douglas the manager and said ' bollocks, fuck it, call it *Rock'n'roll* and we can get out of here and get down to the boozer! **1989**

1916 (1991)
It's like I've written all these anti-war songs and I keep getting accused of being pro-war, right? So I thought I'd write a pro-war one and see if people come out saying it's an anti-war one. **1995**

Some songs take half an hour to write, others take weeks. The fast ones are harder to write. But this time we've come up with a couple of songs that are different, thought nobody will ever believe it. **1991**

'When I was a kid, you waited for the next Beatles album and it was never what you expected. At first, you didn't like it but then you grew to. Well, 1916 is Motörhead's *Revolver*. And I can't wait for our *Sgt. Pepper*. But people just see us as gorillas in leather jackets. **1991**

'It's better than back to form. If it was back to form it's be just another collection of fast numbers. It's the first time I can say that there's no reason except our judgement, that there's anything wrong on that album. We've got exactly what we wanted and everybody's happy

with it. It if fucks up now there's nobody to blame but us, and that's all right by me. **1991**

'I Ain't No Nice Guy' from March Or Die (1992)
We had a hit record on the radio with 'I Ain't No Nice Guy' with Ozzy & Slash on it and Sony actually killed it on purpose because it wasn't their idea. I said to them get it on the AOR playlist, cross it over and they said, "We tried this and we tried that, it's dead" and I said, "You're a fucking liar, you got no fucking time to push it. Forget it, we'll do it." So we got our own people to push it. We got the song and album on the radio and it was high on the playlist, so we went to the label and said, "We got your artist Ozzy on this tune and Slash, let's make a video for the song." And they said, "No". Ozzy and Slash had already agreed to be in the video, so we made our own video for $8,000, eight fuckin' grand!
And then they held it up at MTV until it was dead on the radio. Sony wouldn't sign the release. You know MTV was going to play it, for once they were willing to play one of our records. And then the funny thing is they couldn't because our record company wouldn't let them. Hot Dog! That's stupid as shit. I mean, that's not even the case of not getting behind the band. It's like, how can you afford as a record label to throw away a hit record? **1995**
Bastards (1993)

My favourite is always the newest one, but I especially think *Bastards* is a good one too. **1995**

Sacrifice (1995)
This album's very good. If it were anyone else it'd be Number 1 but because it's Motörhead we're stuck in some sort of heavy metal no man's land. Will it give us a new lease of life in Britain? I don't give a fuck if it doesn't. I'm just doing music I like doing. **1995**

Snake Bite Love (1998)
I don't know that *Snake Bite Love* was one of the worst-selling albums we've ever made, but then again *Everything Louder Than Everyone Else* is one of the best-selling for ages. They're still buying the Motörhead experience and that's all right by me. Lots of recent studio tracks are on there, too. Although others say that the old days were the best ones, I really don't agree. We're playing the best music we've ever played and it's worth getting into, but of course the attention span of the average audience seems to have gone down to about 1.5 seconds. **2000**

I wrote the song 'Snake Bite Love' in 10 minutes. It's an exercise in word association football. It doesn't have to make sense. It's rock'n'roll, isn't it? **1998**

Music In General

've never done demos (laughs). It saves a lot of time and money, you know. We write about five weeks before the initial recording. We write the bare bones of the music, bring them into the studio and work the lyrics out there. **1998**

Motörhead sounds stronger with each new album and there are new fans out there all the time. **1996**

If you forget about your fans, you're forgetting about yourself. **1982**

The audience seems to be getting younger, they'll soon be coming in prams. No, they are getting incredibly young, some of them can't afford to smoke, let alone drink. But it's all the same to me, if they like it - come on! **1982**

You can always make money, you can dig graves or paint skyscrapers. But you can't always make music and please people. **1979**

Forget Art and all that - it's bullshit. If you can sent that shiver down a kid's back, then that's what it's all about. **1979**

For too long a lot of people have regarded us as motorcycle-riding gorillas who play guitars, but actually we are quite intelligent. I've said it before and I'll say it again, if people really like to listen to Motörhead music they will discover that there is a hell of a lot more that just two guitars and drums thrashing away. Often I'll use the bass like a lead instrument. Now that's not easy. **1981**

People say, 'I used to listen to you when I was young'. What the fuck - I was older than you then, anyway! And I'm still doing it and I'm older even, but you look older than me, because you stopped listening to it, right? **1995**

All right, I wouldn't say my voice is beautiful but I think it has character and with the sound it makes I've never had to cancel a gig because of loss of tone. **1981**

We will concentrate on very basic music; loud, fast, city, raucous, arrogant, a paranoid, speed-freak, rock'n'roll... **1976**

There was no master plan. It's really boring to say it, but we write the songs very negligently, we don't do much work on them, we just do whatever we feel at the time. It's that simple. **1991**

Do I write songs on the road? No, not really. We're trying to do that this time, but we aren't doing that real well because we're so fucking lazy. Plus we don't have time at soundcheck 'cos there are two other bands to get up there to check and that wouldn't be fair to them. **1995**

I write words all the time but we write songs in rehearsals before the recording. It's if the mood strikes you. Sometimes you write nothing and sometimes you write 25 and only use five. **1996**

I might get blocked but it doesn't last longer than a couple of days. That's what I've been doing all this time, is writing songs. I'm pretty good at it now. **1996**

We've just been doing what everybody fucking expected us to do, knock off 10 tracks a year and Bob's yer uncle! **1991**

It pisses me off when people say it's the 'usual Motörhead album'. We've never made the 'usual' one.

There's always something different. We experiment, but do it within our own metre, y'know? and it always sickens us that everybody misses it. **2000**

We're more of blues band than a rock'n'roll band. We just play very fast. **1996**

When we hit the road this time (at the end of October 1984) we'll be doing barbershop quartets, and we'll also be wearing candles strapped to our heads. At the end of the shows we'll be swinging out into the audiences with cutlasses between our teeth. We'll swipe at a few heads and then we'll swing back. It will all be very powerful and very entertaining. **1984**

Sex

I'm in the business because I love rock'n'roll and women. I reckon if you can play the guitar you can pull any chick. **1987**

My first shag was fucking disastrous. But I've made up for it since. I was 13. You don't know what the fuck you're doing. You're just hoping for the best and diving in there. It was on a beach, as well. That fucking sand gets everywhere, even under your foreskin. **1998**

The School for the Dancing Arts and Education, Tring, Hertfordshire, mmmmm! Me and this Scottish guy down the Electric Garden, we fucked our way through the entire year, 1968, ha ha ha. Wonderful. Wonderful. All ballet dancers come down to get a bit of rough. Beautiful women, voluptuous, long legs, beautiful naked women pirouetting round the room, with shawls hanging off the ceiling, great stuff. **1991**

There was a lot of fucking going on but it was all very innocent really. That's why today there's a lot of 23-year old guitar players with no visible father, ha ha ha. But there was far more mayhem going on back up in Blackpool; I remember The Tremeloes dumping Lulu in the horse-trough at four in the morning. **1991**

The biggest buzz I've ever got is screwing and going on stage, in varying orders, depending on what I'm going to do next. **1979**

I even lived with Gil Weston for quite a while. When I got her the Girlschool job I said it would break us up, and sure enough it happened six months later. She married the tour chef! **2000**

I'm a slag and I'm 36 years old... I've always been a slag - it's a long time to be a slag, 36 years... but I've had a great time doing it, and I can recommend it to anyone if they can stand the pace... I've been lucky, I can. I'm 36 years old, and I've realised almost every ambition I ever had. **1979**

I've never hung out with men. That's my thing, I like girls. That's the only reason I'm in the music business, I discovered you could get women to take their clothes off if you had a guitar. And they come off a lot faster if you can play it. But all of That's slowed down because of these diseases that God in his infinite wisdom has sent to teach us a lesson. But just before God finally sussed it out, I had a whale of a time.
That's the reason why anybody's in rock'n'roll from that time, if they tell the truth. But they won't. "Oh, I had something to impart to the kids." Fuck off! You wanted to screw that blonde in the fourth form! **1991**

Aids is like the Black Death isn't? But aids isn't going to stop anybody doing anything. There's always something to stop you enjoying yourself isn't there? Getting laid is part of rock, and I'd soon get laid that have to give it up. **1989**

I went with a sex change once, who'd had his dick removed. I figured if he'd had the guts to have his balls and his dick cut off then I had the guts to fuck him. He was female, as long as there isn't a dick, you know what I mean? It was convincing, believe me. Nice tits. Better than most of the girls at the

time. It was at the Embassy Club in Old Bond Street. **2000**

I would have liked to have fucked Madonna before she had the kid. The tits go south don't they? **1998**

The chicks in Estonia, though. Oh, shit yeah. They look like fashion models! All of 'em! Mikkey and I went out the first night, and the club was just jammed with the best looking' women you'd ever seen: blond hair, Finnish or Norwegian, little short skirts, wonderful! That's why I got into rock'n'roll. It has worked for me and I never looked back after that first week after the exams at school. My mother had a guitar lying around the house, and I noticed this guy with a guitar, and he was immediately surrounded by women and I said, "That looks like a good gig." So I took my lumps 'cos I couldn't play, but I was immediately surrounded by chicks. **1995**

I'm fed up with stupid feminists. As far as I'm concerned women still rule because they twist us around their fingers. A truly gorgeous chick doesn't bleat because she knows that she has power over men. **1981**

On the American tours we've done so far, we've been on a bus. It's been finish the gig, get on the bus, and go 1,200 miles. You have to find a young lady who'll come on the bus with you, and then you have to get her a plane back from the next stop. **1982**

We had one chick who was double-jointed dancing with us. She was really dainty and little and blonde, but a sexual pervert of the first order. She'd skip out in this little white dress and roll all her bones out of joint and assume this impossible position. And everyone would go 'Aaaargh!' 'cos they were all tripping. Did I ever cop off with Stacia? No. A lot of people did. I used to share a room with her, and the traffic was amazing. **2000**

We aren't pulling too badly in America. Sometimes I'm quite surprised how well we do. After all, you couldn't call any of us a bronze Adonis.

Wendy O Williams would ring and say, "What are you doing right now? Can I come over and jump you?" And when Wendy O Williams jumped you, you stayed jumped. **2001**

If I die tonight, I can't bitch. I've been all over the world. I've made love to women of all sizes, shapes, colours, creeds and religious persuasions. I've had a great time doing it. **1995**

Lemmy with Christabell, the Countess of Durham, at London's Limelight Club.

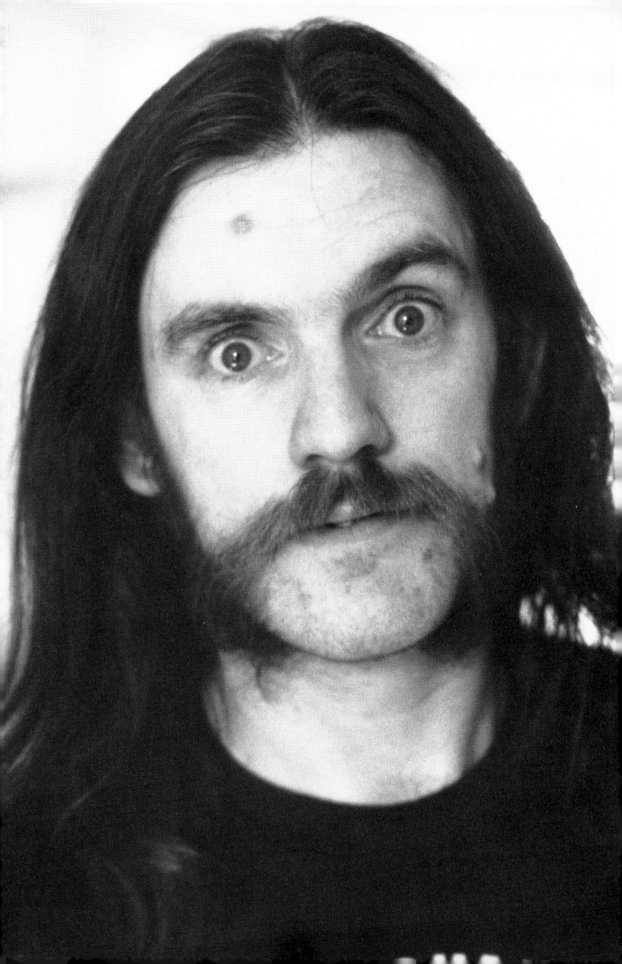

Drugs

Maybe we have the same spirit as the MC5 – but that's because a lot of amphetamines are involved. And the MC5 were well into amphetamines. **1978**

[I was asked] "Do you want to take some LSD?" What the fuck, why not? I thought it might be a bit stronger than dope, and I'd had three joints so I figured I was an authority. He gave me this little white tablet, and I thought, That's small, but I'll eat it anyway, four trips' worth. I was flat on my back for 18 hours, I couldn't do anything. I couldn't move, I couldn't. Kaleidoscope time. **1991**

You can actually do anything on anything if you're used to the effects. But we got spiked with Angel Dust once in Cleveland by two different lots of fucking hippies. That's an interesting drug. It makes you want to jump through car windscreens while they're going along. It's like a lot of these drugs you don't get any more, like Tuinal. They were the replacement for Mandrax, but where it made you dopey, they made you go out and maim people. It was a terrible drug, and if you took one on Friday, by Monday you'd be taking four. **1999**

On speed, even your enemies are imaginary, at least you can see them coming. I've seen people go fucking cracked up and neurotic, but you know, whatever suits you, you should do. It suits me, I do it. **2000**

I love grotty old boozers with blousy old women and beautiful girls. **1979**

I drink about two bottles of vodka a day and of course a few Carlsberg specials. **1981**

Ever taken E? Yeah. I've tried it four times, and nothing ever happened. I think I'm anaesthetised to E by the Hawkwind era. Because back then we were taking real acid, you know... **2000**

When I lived in Manchester in about 1962, there was plenty of dope around in them days. You just had to be in a big city. We used to call it 'shit' and sometimes it was. It was just part of the scene - different from getting pissed, but that's all it was, different. It wasn't worse or better. **1999**

Dealing dope was like selling wine. What side of the hill it grew and so on. And it was true as well. It was better dope in them days, like meth - methyl amphetamine chloride BP with a skull and crossbones on the amp (ampoule). You were supposed to shoot it but I never did: I put it in orange juice and drink it. You could get one of them for 1/9. Last time I saw one it was £150, and that was 10 years ago.

You could get 10 black bombers for a pound and you couldn't give Mandrax away. You could kill yourself real easy in them days. We didn't know how many of us were going to die, it was all new. **1991**

I very rarely sleep. I always wake up tired. I suppose I get about 24 hours sleep a week. **1979**

Speed made you jump about without stopping. I once stayed up for two weeks, and all I had during that time was three blackcurrant pies and two yoghurts. But the best thing was that you could get up on stage when you really didn't feel like it, so it was functional as well as recreational. **1999**

I'm probably nearer to being an alcoholic than I've ever been. I sometimes wake up in the morning lean across the bedside table and pour myself a vodka and orange. Of course, from that point on, the day does tend to slope downwards a bit... **1979**

I think the drug thing has got totally out of control. People are trying everything far too early. They have access to a lot of drugs which are going to bend their minds completely out of shape before they've even got an identity to fall back on if anything gets nasty. **1979**

The first time I was busted was '68. I was living in a house just down the road from the Earl's Court police station where the other guys were dealing a lot of shit around the world. I came home one day and the garden was full of policemen with shovels. Ah, I said, I was just going. And this policeman said, "Don't put your hands in your pockets, son. Let's go inside and see what we can find." **1991**

I was 21 before I took any sort of drug or even really stared drinking. But by then my personality was pretty well formed. **1979**

Aye, two Mandrax capsules. He took me down the station to charge me then offered me a police station mug full of brandy and said Happy New Year. I said "You're fucking nuts!" **1991**

I got busted in a phone box in Fulham Road, with all these blues in me socks. Or was in Dexedrine? Yellows maybe. I sat in the cells in Chelsea nick and ate them one by one. And boy, they tasted rotten. I ate ten, I think. **2000**

What's the longest I've ever been awake? Two weeks. That was the old days, when you could get the good stuff. Liquid meth. You know that Speed Kills thing? That's what they were talking about. Bullshit. It doesn't kill anybody. One and nine for five amps. I put three of 'em in a glass of orange juice. I'll always prefer speed to cocaine. Cocaine makes you think you're gonna throw up, it wears off too quick and you go to sleep on it. What's the point of that? **2000**

When Keith Richards was said to be getting his blood changed, our manager thought this would be a really good idea to get all the toxic shit out of me and start with a clean slate. So we went to my doctor and gave a blood sample. We went back the next day and he said, "Whatever you do, don't change your blood - cos pure blood will kill you!" It had evolved into some sort of organic soup - all kinds of trace elements in it. **1999**

Acid changed me completely. It taught me how to see people and myself a lot better. It was interaction with other people, but the circumstances were different because everyone was a believer and now everyone is not, so I don't think it would be much fun any more. But my worst drug experience was the only bad trip I ever had. It involved breathing in the dark which I can't really describe, but it wasn't nice. **1999**

I've never been interested in cocaine. I don't like it and I've never bought it. You spend a lot of time laughing out of context and it makes people really paranoid. We used to go and see this cocaine dealer, and he was always by the window looking out of the edge of the curtains. He had a huge apartment and he never seemed to be in any of it, just by the window. One day I asked him what the fuck he was looking for and he said I don't

know, but they're out there man. And then he said the funniest thing I've ever heard anybody say on drugs. **1999**

I think Lou Reed should burn in hell for the amount of people he's got into heroin through that song ('Heroin'). **1999**

My girlfriend died of heroin in 1973. I wasn't very keen on trying it anyway, because I'd seen people turn into grovelling dogs on it. I wasn't gonna do anything that made you that desperate, especially considering how much it costs, and I was right. The thing with junkies is, they have to want to stop and you can't make them if they don't. And needles are evil. That's an addiction in itself. **1999**

Okay, I admit I'm a bit of a speed freak, but I never touch smack. Besides, people who like smack also like Lou Reed, and that can't be anything in its favour. **1972**

I was in the music business without drugs first. But not for long, because I moved to London and everyone was doing acid. There wasn't peer pressure: I just felt like doing it to see why everyone was laughing all the time. See, the drugs make you feel good, right? That's why people take them. They don't take them because their friends are taking them, or because the evil pusher's waiting outside school in an ice cream van. The reason they do it is because they tried it once and it was fucking great, so they do it again. it's the same as alcohol. If people do something and they like it, then want more, and there's nothing you can do about it. That's human nature, it's no good busting users or dealers, because it's a social thing. People want drugs and they will get them, so you might as well regulate it so you can tax the motherfucker. I can't understand why people are so fucking stupid as to put kids in jail for smoking a few joints. They come out as fully-fledged homosexual safe-breakers. Good thinking. It's fucking insane. **1999**

I read something the other day that said 60 per cent of the people in America's jails are there on drug charges. Half of them are first offenders and nearly all of them are for non-violent crimes. It's a fucking joke! A rapist gets out quicker! People should stop persisting with this terrible bogeyman of drugs in the public eye, 'cos if they ever wanted to legalise the public outcry would stop them. It's very, very foolish. I mean, even the generation who are making all these law did drugs! Yeah, right, Clinton didn't inhale and he had a blow-job and didn't come. He got a good record for not doing things. **1999**

The only thing I ever saw anyone die on was heroin or downers. I never saw anyone die of speed, coke or marijuana. So it you wanna die kids, take heroin. If you don't then take something else.

But I truly believe that if you can do without then you're better off. I hate to give advice because I'm 53, I'm their parents age so they think, What's that old cunt know? But I do know, believe me. I fucking know. **1999**

They charged me with coke, but it was speed so they threw it out of court. But I was - guilty of getting caught! **1996**

I've seen God on acid - he's taller. **1996**

I never did heroin or anything like that. That's something you can't use because it stops you from taking care of business. It stops your breathing too. People don't understand that because they think people who are older than them, know nothing. We're all just old, dumb and finished. They're the new brave, young breed and it won't happen to them. They think they're smarter but heroin is smarter than everybody. **1996**

They say acid doesn't work two days in a row, but if you double the dose it does! **1999**

Too many people fall for fucking heroin. I can't believe it, you know? It's like there's not enough dead bodies yet to persuade you that it may not be such a good idea after all. How many people do we have to have dead before they're 20? **1998**

Rock'n'Roll

I don't recommend my lifestyle. It's been finely tuned over a long time. It would kill most people. **1998**

We're a rock'n'roll band, man, you should come see us, you go away knowing you've seen some rock'n'roll. No doubt about that. **1999**

For me rock music is all about going out on a Saturday night, getting drunk, being sick down your thread and pulling a bird - although not necessarily in that order. **1981**

People only change 'cos they think they should. We're happy as we are. We wanna be like Status Quo and go on forever. Chuck Berry never changed. Little Richard never changed. I'd rather be like that and stick to a formula we're happy with. We're not gonna be like Slade or Def Leppard. **1982**

I happen to think that the buzz that music gives you can be better than screwing. I mean, women get old and mangy but records don't. A good piece of music will always take you high even if you haven't heard it for years. **1981**

You couldn't do this if you didn't like it, it's not an easy life. The schedules are punishing, physically and mentally. You've got to believe, and I believe completely in rock'n'roll. It still makes you feel like you can face going back to the factory for another week, which is more or less what it's for, it's fun, rebellion for its own sake. That's the idea of rock'n'roll. Once you get respectable rock'n'roll, it's not rock'n'roll any more. **1998**

Don't mention the Angels, best not to. You don't know what they're going to take exception to. And you wouldn't like it, believe me. People thought we were a biker band. But I haven't had a bike since I was 16, a 1940s ex-Army Matchless, a fucking old puffer. **1991**

If people listened to more rock'n'roll and less Margaret Thatcher or Michael Foot or Roy Jenkins... In fact, if the bits of their brains that wanted to be politicians could be exterminated, and the bit that would've liked rock'n'roll

somehow could be artificially enlarged, wouldn't it be more fun to be around them? **1979**

We are the rock'n'roll lifestyle. If life ain't fun, you might as well be dead. The human race needs people like us. They won't let me smoke on TV. Because of course, if some kid sees me smoking, of course they'll want to buy some too. Fucking stupid. I've done everything except smack and that's why I'm alive and all my mates are dead. **1991**

I try to do a bottle of whisky a day. Whether I need it or not. **1998**

It's not an ideal job for an enduring, committed, caring relationship, because on the road your main objective is to get fucked all the time: in the back of the bus, under the bus, on top of the bus, in the dressing room, in the grass outside. And, given that, the bird feels a bit uneasy when you're away for three months. **1998**

Rock'n'roll was not made to sell. It was made for joy. That's the reason for rock'n'roll. It's not that you can be a millionaire doing it. Oh yeah, a big Cessna fucking plane and a car and a yacht - it's got nothing to do with it. It's if you can get laid, right? That is what rock'n'roll is about. It's about outraging your parents, pissing off the entire neighbourhood and getting laid! **1995**

It's death for them usually. After an interview with me, people have come out of a boozer on their hands and knees. **1998**

Brian Robertson, Lemmy & Phil Taylor.

I drink a bottle of Bourbon a day, but I don't get falling-down drunk. I don't even grab for the banisters much these day 'cos after the earthquake in LA I've got no faith in them. **1996**

I'm trying to give them that feeling I first felt the first time I heard 'All Shook Up' or 'Golly Miss Molly'. I just want to send that shiver up their back because it's the best thing I ever felt. It's even better than screwing. **1979.**

I ain't threatening nobody, I'm just observing a few things. I ain't got no answers, I just got lots of questions and they never answer any of them. The most dangerous thing is that all these radio stations and MTV will like be scared of them, that's the dangerous thing because that leaves you no recourse, you know, except to be more threatening. If they would play a fair amount of everything, then it would be okay because then kids could make up their own minds. But they won't. **1996**

People think you're a hoodlum with your leather jacket on. **1995**

Bullshit. It's rock'n'roll. I remember it before metal or punk. I came up with Elvis Presley and Little Richard the first time round. They got no right to put me into a thing that came up twenty years later. Fuck' em, I don't fit into any category. I'm Lemmy and I play what I play and that's it. That's the only category I'll accept. **1996** I'll play what the fuck I want. I was raised on early rock'n'roll and The Beatles, where you did anything you liked. Every time a Beatles LP came out, it was like a different band. You had to really work on liking it and it was worth it too because you found different things in there. I don't want to be obvious. Fuck 'em. **1996**

You're supposed to have fun with rock'n'roll. What's it for otherwise? **1996**

If it wasn't for this? If it weren't for rock'n'roll, how would we exist? We'd be thieves. **1983**

They're trying to kill rock'n'roll again. They're not going to do it. They tried before with Elvis and The Beatles. Burn your Beatle memorabilia, pick up points all over the south. It really didn't work that well did it? It's not going to work this time either. There are bands out here that are playing and the fans go to watch them. It's no different. Everything is just fine. It's only the media who say it's dead. I don't see any people on the street saying it's fuckin' dead. They still come to the concerts and tell me that I've changed their lives and shit. **1996**

The South American market is really big now. Iron Maiden, Skid Row and us played to 56,000 in Sao Paulo three or four weeks ago. I wouldn't say rock'n'roll is dead. If it dies over here, we can go over there 'til it revives itself. America should be ashamed of those statistics. One reason for this is that everybody plays video games today because the tickets are out priced. They're pricing themselves out of the fuckin' market. They're cutting their own throats. **1996**

Phil, Lemmy and 'Fast' Eddie.

Some of the kids stay all through the gig with their heads pressed right up against the speakers. They may be injuring themselves, but it's their heads they're putting in there. I feel no responsibility whatsoever. Anyway, how can we stop them? They keep shouting 'turn it up, turn it up, louder, louder'. **1979**

Motörhead v The Music Biz

The Stiff Records thing was the real pisser, because our single was sidelined while they put out things like Plummet Airlines, a real obvious hit. But I'm used to not being appreciated by the business. The business has demonstrated year in, year out, that it knows nothing about rock'n'roll. It's not even interested in finding out. I didn't join the business, I joined the band, and although it won't admit it, I've beaten it hand over fist every time. They always do whatever I tell them not to, and they always fuck up. **2000**

I'll tell you what gets me down and that's people like the *New Musical Express* and the way they're always running heavy metal down and saying it's not going anywhere. They must be fucking stupid. What they should be writing about is what the kids are doing. Thousands of kids like heavy metal and popular music is what it's supposed to be about. **1982**

They can't stand it even now. We're like a hot wire up their bums and I love it. **1980**

Once you've been in this business for three years, it gets in your blood. You can't do anything else. **1984**

Gerry Bron (Bronze Records boss) signed us as a favour, but he went on to release five of our albums, so that's one helluva favour. So, again, fuck you! **2000**

SPV knew we wouldn't let 'em have any input from day one, but Epic always wanted to drop by the studio and hear what we were doing. In the end I had to say to the guy, "We're trying to make a record, would you mind fucking off? I don't come to your office telling you how to type." He got the message. **2000**

We made it without the critics, we made it in spite of the critics, if the kids like it then they'll keep coming to the shows. I'm doing it to be David Bowie. I'm doing it to have good gigs and that's it. Have a good time at a Motörhead gig, that's all I'm preaching. DATE?

You bastards are never gonna tell me what I can fucking sing about. **1996**

[In the video we made for Killed By Death]… I put my hand on the girl's leg while she was on the motorbike. I ran it up out of sight and they thought that it meant that I grabbed her fanny, you know? I mean what the fuck do they think that I'm gonna do with this chick, stop and have a cup of tea at a roadside cafe. I mean what the fuck are they talking about? I mean if you get a girl on a motorbike and you're rolling down the road, you're gonna fuck her. I mean, that's the story. What are they scared of? **1996**

That bloke from *Time Out* just destroyed *We Are Motörhead* with personal attacks. But I should be used to it by now, I've seen reviews of our concerts that mention songs we didn't even play. The writers must have been in the bar with their set-lists, not watching the show. Useless cunts - how dare they?! **2000**

They (Sony) won't spend any money to promote the fucking albums, and then they blame the band for not selling records. Then they fire us off the label, fuckin' stupid bastards. **1995**

Last year, Sony spent three million promoting Michael Jackson. I mean, he really needed promoted, right? Hell, just put him on a talk show and say the new album's out and people go buy it. Shit, it doesn't make too much sense to spend all that money because it's such a bad album. **1995**

Very happy so far with CMC. We didn't get involved in that Castle project. They didn't ask us they just went ahead. They own it now having bought all those tracks from Bronze. We can't do nothing. Oh, yeah we'll get royalties. They just bought the whole catalogue off Bronze. **1996**

The worst nightmare was Sony, no doubt. We got nominated for a Grammy for our first Epic album, 1916, and I went to New York for the ceremonies and Tommy Mottola never even came out and said hello. **1998**
You would think that being

nominated for a Grammy would rise you above the house, and be in the 'signed for life' level. But no, not a chance – it didn't help. Nothing helps, you just have to go on just plodding through it. I believe it's just making us better people or some fucking shit. It's probably because of that we are still around. You know because we are so pissed off which is very good for a band, the force of it. **1998**

I had a great speech ready in the event we had won (a heavy metal Grammy). I was going to say, "I'm not going to thank anybody. None of you fuckers have ever given us a hand. You didn't do anything. We did it all by ourselves. Thank you very much. Good night." **1996**

There are masses of people who spread their views on us without even having heard anything by us in their lives. I have met people who have told me, "I wouldn't like your type of music anyway, That's why I have never listened to it." Pure arrogance! **1999**

Maybe Sony felt they were getting the 'Grandfathers of Thrash', and they weren't. They were getting an extremely opinionated older guy and three younger geezers who were worse! **1992**

Ages ago, we had the 'No Sleep 'Til Hammersmith' tour. The last gig was at the Odeon and we had *Kerrang!* written across the top in capital letters. about a year later,

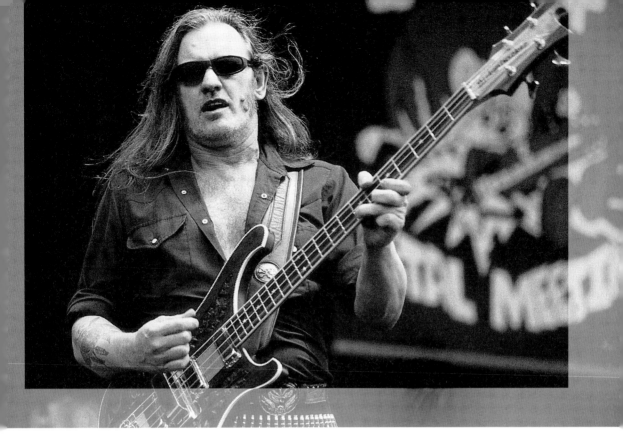

Kerrang! magazine came out. I'd have thought they would have had us on the cover a bit more seeing as they stole the name. **1988**

I don't mean to appear bitter because I'm actually having a great time in my life, but you're asking some very specific things. Fuck the record company and fuck everybody who tells you to do things a certain way, because you're the only one who knows your heart or your soul. Believe me, they can steal your money but they can never steal your heart or your belief. **2000**

People see the name Motörhead and they don't hear it because they don't play it, they don't even go near it. That's our problem. The label CMC International Records can only hope it gets played, and me too. It's been shopped around to radio stations and as I said some will play it and others won't. **1996**

It's just business as usual. I expect the record business to be assholes, because that's their job. It's run by accountants now. As long as an accountant is running anything, the degree of quality goes straight out the window. The label on the Del Monte spinach can hasn't changed in a long time. Just the way the accountants like it: "Change the label? Do you have any idea how much that would cost?!?!?" But I couldn't give a fuck. They can't hurt me. They can't stop me. I've demonstrated that. Now it's time to rock the boat a little. Because the boat stinks at the moment. **1995**

Motörhead and Girlschool, left to right:
Denise Dufort, Lemmy, Kelly Johnson,
Phil Taylor, Enid Williams,
'Fast' Eddie and Kim McAuliffe.

There have been no significant advances with the situation. We're just trying to get out of the (Bronze) deal, because we don't think they're promoting us. I'm sick to death of it, we can't do anything. We can't do any recording, we can't look for another label, all we can do is go on stage, and that's it. Their lawyers are writing our lawyers letters back at £100 a day. Businessmen always fuck everything up. **1985**

We put our lives on the line, same as you do as a journalist, right? I'd like to see those businessmen do that. The longer I've been in the record business the less respect I have for them. They're just assholes. **1985**

United Artists didn't know how to market the first LP. Motörhead don't fit into any category, really. We're not a straight heavy metal, because we're a rock'n'roll band, which no one knows how to market any more. They didn't know even then. A straight rock'n'roll band isn't that interesting, although we could have become interesting if they'd let us. We could have burned down a few large buildings or something. I don't know, they just didn't think it was musical. United Artists were a bunch of twats in the final analysis. **2000**

The funny thing is over here (in America), each album's been more ignored than the last one, because the record company (BMG) ain't doing their job. Well, why should they? And if you think of it from their point of view, they've had Motörhead for three albums and they ain't selling millions, so fuck 'em. I suppose that's what they do here. But anyway, we'll keep on making albums until they buy 'em. I'll stare 'em down. **1999**

Record companies are a hindrance to rock'n'roll, not a help. They dilute the real thing down to the lowest common denominator. **2000**

Lemmy and drummer Pete Gill , who replaced Phil Taylor in 1983.

Media Matters

The logo came from Joe Petagno who did a lot of our sleeves. He doesn't do much record sleeve work, just us really. He does mostly advertising and lives in Copenhagen. It was designed to stick. I always knew that. In the Sixties you had The Yardbirds and The Moody Blues who all wrote their names a certain way, and if you had that name written you could see it even when you couldn't read it. Like a British rail logo, a swastika, anything like that, you see the symbol, and you don't have to write the name. **1989**

Who gives a fuck if major corporations like Coors and 7-Up are supporting and even bankrolling the efforts of groups like the PMRC? I don't drink 7-Up anyway, and don't drink Coors because it's shit beer. **1996**

You act nice and they think you're weak. Everybody shakes your hand, buys you a bottle of booze and then they go behind your back and fuck you over. The only option is physical force, which I hate because I'm not into violence. We may have got ourselves a bad name through that, but sometimes there's no other way to get results. **2000**

If you want to see obscenity in America it's not a pair of tits on MTV, it's those bastards on Sundays. Get some poor widow to send 'em in ten bucks and then she dies from hypothermia because she can't afford to put the fucking heat or electric power on. But they don't give a shit about that, they take the ten bucks and smile. **1996**

I think Mark Lamarr (host of TV's *Never Mind The Buzzcocks*) is a jumped-up little cunt. He sits there and drags everyone else down to make himself look big. For a start, I noticed him rehearsing all the ad-libs for an hour before the show. And I wouldn't join in. I said, "Fuck it, if it's an ad-lib you don't practice it." So they didn't like that, they had the knives out.

Then these four birds came on, one of whom was that chick out of Bucks Fizz. That Jay bird. And they fucking laid

Mark Lamarr

67

them chicks, and the chicks hadn't even got a mike to defend themselves. "Didn't I see you down the whorehouse?" and all this shit. Really Neanderthal stuff. And I just said, "Fuck it, I don't have to sit here on this rubbish fucking show." I got up and fucked off. They cut the show to make it seem that I didn't split. But I did. **2000**

Never Mind The Buzzcocks is run by an oily little shit. And a fatboy. They rehearse all them ad-libs for two hours before the show. I should've fucking closed it right there. Rehearsing ad libs is not my style. **2000**

"… My bed's a mess of rattlesnakes". Some chick in the *Melody Maker* in England said that was a sexist song. She took it all very seriously. There's no joy in her life, is there? No whimsicality at all. All she sees is doom, feminism and food. So fuck her. **1996**

Gotta have a sense of humour or you're dead. These people nowadays, the politically correct, they have no sense of humour. What the fuck is politically correct, anyway? Do you know what they call Chernobyl now? "A super-prompt critical power excursion." Makes it sound like they're at the fuckin' beach. Nuclear meltdown is what you want to call it, that's what it was. **1996**

If nobody listens to the censors, they're dead, right? And all these radio stations if they just said "Fuck you" they'd be fucked. What could they do? If nobody listened to them they couldn't do a damn thing, right? I'll keep on playing until I die, and we never got any radio play anyway. **1996**

I got a phone call that woke me up telling me the news that we were Number 1. It was a shock even to me, despite my being quite arrogant back then. I just told the guy to call me back the next day when I was awake so he could tell me about it. **1998**

Lemmy with Wurzel and Phil Campbell.

Head Gear
(Guitars, Amps, etc)

Marshalls changed rock'n'roll as much as any band. **1997**

Really, all the collateral I've got in the world is two Marshall stacks, three Rickenbacker guitars and a collection of ashtrays. **1981**

I started in 1959 doing instrumental stuff and Shadows walks, that sort of thing. The first guitar I has was a Hofner Club 50 and then I got a horrendous Eko guitar, silver glitter with about four pickups on it. Then I traded it in, no, actually I didn't trade it in, it was so fucking awful that nobody would take it! So the next guitar was the old one-pickup semi-acoustic Harmony Meteor, a really nice guitar. Next was a Gibson 330, the one with the silver-coloured pickups with the little triangles on them, and eventually I traded that in for a maple-necked Telecaster.
By the time I joined the Rockin' Vicars they had a group guitar, which was a Fender Jazzmaster. I really hated the neck on it, but it had a fantastic sound so I swapped the neck from the Tele to the Jazzmaster and that became the best guitar I've ever seen in my life. That was some box, because you could do all flash runs on the Tele neck, but the pickups on the Jazzmaster were so much better. Eventually I was with Sam Gopal, and instead of royalties they gave

us each a guitar. I had this old Firebird VII, a 1963 one which was unbelievable, probably the best guitar I've ever owned. I lent it to a friend and he sold it to buy himself another guitar – some friend! **1982**

The Rickenbacker I've still got now is a really old one with a Gibson Thunderbird pickup on it. I'm still using it, a furious monster of a thing. It sounds amazing with that pickup. I had a real Thunderbird once, but that got nicked as well, haven't had a lot of luck have I? The Ricky is an old Mono one, not the stereo 4001, although I've got a couple of them as well. I've had the head replaced recently, found a crack at the back of it, it's had a bit of rough treatment in its time. **1982**

I've got an old 4x12 (speaker cabinet) that I've had for years, one of the straight-fronted ones, and a 4x15 which is much better than an 18. I've got a great stack of Marshall gear, but basically it's the same as it's been for years, two stacks with two heads, bass Marshalls, old ones, 4x12s and the 4x15s. There's a new amplifier I've got, it's called 'No Morals', I've started cutting up the lettering on Marshalls and seeing what I can turn the name into. One's called Marsha, one's called Arsall and there's my favourite, No Morals, that was a particularly inspired one, that! **1982**

I play a lot of notes, but I also play a lot of chords. And I play a lot of open strings. I just don't play like a bass player. There are complaints about me from time to time. It's not like having a bass player; it's like having a deep guitarist. **1995**

I have seven Rickenbacker basses but I only use one. It's the new one. Rickenbacker is bringing out the signature Lemmy bass which I designed and it's the most beautiful thing you've ever seen in your life! It's all carved on the front with oak leaves and stuff and they're bringing that out soon. I've got the first one and Rickenbacker has finally made some good pickups! It sounds like murder. **1998**

Do I play through guitar amps? No, they're old Marshalls, and Super Bass 2 JMPs, 'cos I don't like those JCM 800s. They're worth fuck all. Jim Marshall sent me two free stacks. I put 'em back in the boxes and sent 'em back to him. Fuckin' crap they are. Still, he's doin' good; he made a lot of money sellin' 'em. Everyone has a JCM 800, but they're garbage. He used 'em for ages (pointing to Phil) then he stopped putting up with them and threw 'em out. We're gonna try and get him an old stack. **1995**

I'm such a mediocre guitarist. I'm good at rhythm, but I was never any good at lead. I do the odd guitar thing here and there, but I forgot most of the notes or what little I really did know. **1995**

I'm not fucking Hendrix - who is? But I've got a good right hand - I learned to play rhythm really well. A lot of the new heavy rock groups, a lot of kids learn to play solos but they can't play rhythm to save their life, and without that you've got nothing. Just a lot of wanking. **1999**

I learned to play bass on stage with Hawkwind 'cause I never played bass in my life. I knew the guitarist because he took eight tabs of acid and then we never saw him for five years. He vanished, then returned in Widowmaker. So anyway, they lost a guitar player, and I showed up looking for a job, and they wanted a speed freak in the band.

He wanted me to join, so he took me with him to this festival. It turns out they didn't need another guitarist, 'cause Dave Brock decided to play lead, so I was fucked.
But the bass player never showed up, so he told me to play bass. I go out on stage with this bass around my neck, and it was a Rickenbacker, too. The bass player, like an idiot, left his bass in the truck. So I'm learning. Nik Turner says to make some noises in E. 'This one's called 'You Shouldn't Do That.' Then he walks away… **1995**

I'm not a rhythm guitarist , I'm not a bassist. I'm not anything, really. I'm me. I'm what I do. I'm not categorisable. **1996**

I think my hearing is okay. The human body adapts remarkably well to a lot of abuse. I've never used earplugs. Earplugs are for Ted Nugent. How could you expect the audience to stand something that you will not? **2000**

I've got two stacks on stage, both house 4x15s & 4x12s and on top of that I've got two Marshall's JNP Super Bass tube 100 watt amps. **1996**

At home, I've got a great Gibson, a very old 1902 Epiphone Triumph, an old Gibson with just a little 'f' hole in the front. I don't remember what model it is. And I've got a Mitchell Jumbo, she's very nice. **1998**

Nazi Chic

Of wars, World War II is the most interesting one because of the Nazi thing. I just got a new book by this guy who found some archives. It turns out that the head of the Gestapo was supposedly killed in Berlin in 1945. Well, they dug up his grave a few years ago, and there were three people in it. None of them were him. He has apparently been working for the CIA since 1948. **1995**

Nazi Germany is my subject; I'm an expert, especially on the Waffen SS. I could tell you some weird stuff. Bad guys are always more interesting. **1991**

No, I'm not a Nazi. I have two black girlfriends in this city, so I must be the worst Nazi you ever came across. Half of my Jewish friends and black friends can go in my apartment and not be bothered by it. What's the problem with the Nazi thing? The Nazis are gone. Gone. The only reason they ever made it was Hitler. The day after he shot himself they sued for peace. It was just him. Nothing else. There wasn't an ideology that lasts for a thousand years, as has been proved. People have tried to start it up again all over the world and it's not worked. **2000**

I'll explain it in an unusual way for you, right? An SS Honour dagger, if you could find one these days, is worth $200,000. This is not your material that skinheads would buy, right? This is doctors and dentists. It is now antique - material from an age that has gone by and will never rise again, because the whole thing behind the Nazi party is that without Hitler there is nothing. I am the furthest thing from a Nazi you could imagine. I have no racial prejudice whatsoever. Show up at a Nuremberg rally, and I don't think Hitler would've been shaking my hand.

Hitler didn't drink or smoke. Vegetarian. Nice smart uniform, nice short hair. Perfect guy. Accepted completely in any American home, right now. And he slaughtered a quarter of the world. Any questions? **1996**

People are weird, aren't they? They'll say anything. You should never, ever listen about anybody from anybody else excepts themselves, 'cos you don't know. People will say any fuckin' thing. They say that I was a Nazi. It's really weird. There are very few people less Nazi than me on the face of the earth. So I thought I'd wind people up and dress up like one cause that really gets them. I've got three girlfriends in LA and they're all black. If they can get along with what I got in my house, you ain't got nothing to talk about at all. My manager's half Jewish and half Italian, so that takes care of that. There's no way that someone that writes a song like '1916' is a Nazi. **1996**

Everybody likes tyrants. Everybody likes to read about the great tyrants and fucking genocides of history. You don't want to hear about medieval agrarian fucking reform, do you? You want to hear about Attila The Hun, right? And Genghis Khan. They're much more fun. Napoleon. He was called, incidentally, the 'Beast Of Europe', because he was supposed to rape Belgian nuns. **2000**

I insisted the Bomber sleeve should be a German plane. Sure, it's a filthy memory - but the fact is bad guys make the best shit. The Spitfire was a very beautiful aircraft, but the Messerschmitt looked like it was built to kill. Wartime accelerates progress - you better get it out, or the cunt will shoot you. Anyway, the band

should have been rather smaller to get the scale right.Mötley Crüe stole the Germanic imagery thing from us, but then again, I nicked it from Blue Öyster Cult, even down to the Umlaut.' **2000**

I never got on with (Robert) Calvert. He was barmy. He once went for me with a sword on stage. But I did pick up on the Luftwaffe interest, it's true. And I also stole the riff for Motörhead from the first track (of his 'Captain Lockheed And The Starfighters') You keep you eyes and ears open, don't you? **2000**

I'm interested in the Second World Was as a social phenomenon. I fell in love with the uniform, and I will say it now, I don't care, the Swastika is the greatest design that has ever been. It can hit you from five miles away, it's strong. See that Brazilian flag up there? That's strong too, isn't it? I'm taking designs here – not ideologies. **1989**

Lemmy with Brian Robertson and Phil Taylor.

Lemmy In Exile

I see us being successful mainly in America, because there's more scope there – more room in the States to do whatever you're doing and get accepted. Over here, there's only one fashion at a time, and it you haven't got that fashion you get lost in the crush. **1978**

I love America, actually. I'd quite happily move here tomorrow. The thing I dislike about Europe is that it's always rainy and there's so much grey brick. **1982**

The first time I ever went to Los Angeles I liked it. I think it's the palm trees. I just like LA 'cos it's America, and my generation was very Americanised. You don't get any of this high-blown bullshit of people is stupid suits, besides which, I'm much more popular with American women that I am with British women. It's ludicrous anyway. How can you sell out by moving anywhere? If I moved to Scotland no one would say I sold out. The bigger deal is that we've come in with a better album than we've made in our lives.
To wind up this thing about LA, nobody buys our albums here anyway. Now we can go to LA and come back with tans and everything and everyone treats us like a foreign band. Oh, you're interesting now. Everyone's falling over their arse to do an interview now. **1991**

LA is a very funny place. It has no people who are natives. Everybody is moved there from somewhere else. Second and third generation LA people are very weird, 'cos they've never see anything but sunshine, except for two weeks of torrential rain in January, so they tend to be a bit light-headed. But it's a good place. You never get bored. I was bored shitless of London; 44 years is enough, I feel. I had to go somewhere. It didn't have to be LA. **1998**

People don't like me living in LA, and I don't understand it – I wasn't exactly around their house all the time! **1993**

If you're disdainful of the human race in general, what better place to live than LA? A constant source of material. But I quite like America, you see. I mean, apart from all the violence and everything, which is endemic to most Western states, it's fun. I think it's much more fun to live on the edge, and you're certainly on the edge in LA. You get out on the street of an evening, and you realise you really shouldn't have. **2000**

I live in the middle of a gay community, which is up on Sunset, West Hollywood. They think I'm all right, I s'pose. The landlord went around with a petition trying to get me evicted five years ago, and they all wouldn't sign it. But California's kind of a drag right now because they banned smoking everywhere. You can't smoke in any bar in California. You can go out on the patio like a whipped dog, but I've never been much of a whipped dog fancier, really. So we smoke in there anyway until they throw us out. You go into a lot of boozers of an evening that way. **2000**

I've always liked America. The great thing is you can play here for three years and never play the same place twice. **1982**

Weird English, everything embarrasses us. Being caught outside, being caught inside. Things embarrass Americans but they just talk louder to cover up. **2001**

There's a lot of violence over here (America), I think all the sunshine boils you brain. **1982**

On Stage

I nearly fell off the stage last night, stepped forward to do my superstar pose act right onto this packing case on wheels which was the same height as the stage. I skated across the floor on one leg. The other was still on the stage. I thought "This is it, I'm going to die a terrible death and crash to the floor" but I managed to make it part of the act. See clever Lemmy pretend to fall off the stage. **1977**

It's very difficult to replace the Bomber, but then again we knew that we couldn't go lugging the bloody thing around with us all our lives. We'll use it in America because they haven't seen it and I think it will screw their heads up seeing that thing swinging about above their heads. **1982**

I like dressing in the same socks for three weeks running, pedalling out there and raising the trammelled face to the rafters and croaking out 'Ace Of Spades' again. You look out into the crowd and see the face of just one kid who's gone. That's wonderful; it makes it all worth it. **1991**

I'm half drunk when I go on stage and completely blasted when I come off. **1981**

Ideally we'd like to get a six foot tall Amazon in twice a week to swab the place down and then give us a good thrashing. **1984**

This American tour is strictly temporary. There's no way we'll forget the kids in England. We'll be trying our hardest to be back touring. And that's a promise. **1982**

What we do is very hard. Somebody worked out once that the amount of energy we expend on stage in ninety minutes is the same as a Canadian lumberjack uses in a week. **1981**

The last time I had a cramp in my hand and I had to have the pick taped to my finger for the whole gig was pretty embarrassing. **1996**

Somebody threw a fish-gutting knife at me, open, with a curved blade. Another three a bandolier of brass cartridges, this long. At Donington somebody threw one of those burning torches they use on the motorways when it's foggy. It nearly hit Phil Campbell and that stuff sticks to you and burns. I was going to stop the show there and walk off.
These kids came up to me six months later in the boozer and they said, "You know that guy who threw that thing at you at Donington? We kicked the shit out of him." And that, basically, is what it comes down to. The audience must police itself. If our fans see anybody trying to throw things at us, stop 'em. Give us some support. **1989**

I'm on iffy ground as far as technical expertise goes, I'm not the best bass player by a long shot. But the audience can believe in me. I can talk to them and they can tell what I say isn't bullshit. Unlike someone like Ted Nugent who can say things like "Ooooh I can see a load of rock'n'roll hound dogs out there, woof, woof, woof" - that's terrible, that's really crass. **1982**

We've had one group picketing once, it was the Mohicans for Jesus it was. How about that, huh? All these bozos carried Mohicans for Jesus signs

saying, "Don't go in here, it's the voice of the devil." I mean for Christ's sake you really think the devil looks like me? I'm sure he's better looking. **1996**

We went to Canada, Argentina, Chile and all over Europe, including Estonia for the first time. And Poland. Never been to Poland before. I don't know if we'll be going again. It's miserable there; not much fun. It's a funny country. I got strange vibes over there. It was weird. Some of them were really friendly. They were really good people. **1995**

Off Duty

The old man likes *Pirates Of Penzance* more than fucking Motörhead. It ain't their cup of tea, but they pretend to like it. They're just glad I've got a job for Christ's sake. **1998**

My mum calls me Ian, that's about it. Even my father calls me Lemmy now. **1998**

I don't see how you can get sick of enjoying yourself - I haven't so far, and I'm damn sure I resent anyone who tells me I should. Just have a good time and don't hurt anyone else doing it. **1979**

What you see is what you get, man. I've only got one pair of pants and I've had them for 25 years. Nobody knows that. They think I get new pairs but I just paint the holes in my legs black. **1999**

Do you know something? I've got about six left white boots because I wear the right ones out first, right? And I would only wear one pair at a time, you know? So if you know any fucking one-legged, left-footed dancers, ask them to get in touch. They might be really glad of these. Mint condition. **1999**

A woman mistook me for Willie Nelson on the plane from Texas once. It was a night flight out of, fucking, I-don't-know-where-we-were, Corpus Christi, and this woman said, "Do y'all play country and western or what?" I said, "No we don't." "Oh... only y'all look so much like Willie Nelson." What!? I really need this shit in the middle of the night! I knew that she was nervous about landing, so I made the crack to her about cartwheeling down the runway in a ball of fire, loudly, as we landed! **1995**

I will meet any amount of fans at gigs. I just ask them to be polite. I don't like people taking you for granted. I share my stuff with them and they should be respectful of that. I'm not asking people to bow down, but some people take the piss. "Remember me at Chester, 12 years ago?" Then you have to go off and have a drink with them and meet their parents. I don't wanna do that! **1989**

I'm good with words, my vocabulary's good. My vocabulary has improved a lot since the band started through doing lyrics, and also because I've got older. I devour books, me, I eat them for breakfast. I got three books going at a time. I love descriptive writing, and English is the greatest descriptive language in the world. You can have ten words that mean the same thing, but with a little twist on it, French is the next one, but English is pretty good. I'd like to write but I don't have the patience, at least I don't think I have. I can't type, and I couldn't be bothered to do it longhand. **1989**

I'm very Buddha, me, I sit and watch the shit go by. **2000**

Authority

Fighting doesn't mean shit to me. Oh, I took a gun off a geezer over here. He drove by in a van and me and this bird were waiting for the lights to change. He shouted something and she said, "Fuck off, creep", and the van pulled over and he got out with this big silver 45 automatic. He looked like he was going to shoot her. So I just reached out and took the gun out of his hand. What are you gonna do? See the chick get shot? I was thinking, "I'm going to die now. Fucking hell." **2000**

The authorities are frightened of change, but the change is gonna happen whether they like it or not. I mean it's just too bad, right? I don't like some of the things that are happening right now, but I ain't gonna bitch about it because it's part of the natural cycle. So they're fighting against themselves in trying to stop it, because as soon as they try, the kids go straight for it. **1996**

Your life is as stimulating intellectually as your intellect can handle. If band can't think of anything else to do but be morons, them I'm afraid they're stuck with it. We go places that people only dream of visiting. You get to meet people on their own turf. If you ask me, it's stupid to go abroad and go to an English pub. Eating cheese and onion crisps in fucking Barcelona. Eat some paella, see how they do it. Then you'll know more about the world. **1998**

I've seen a lot of politicians come and go and they're all the same mealy-mouthed bastards, kissing fucking babies and shaking hands with hard hats and shit and everybody knows that it's a game and they still play it. Why? There are better games now! You can play all kinds of games on video. Make a game of it, right? The TV whoever shoots the most fucking space ships, then he gets to be president. Makes as much sense as all that rigmarole you go through for a year before the election, right? **1995**

I think marriage is very irrational. It was invented when we were all living in fucking mud huts. Nowadays, everybody cheats on everybody but the married people say then don't, which is rank bullshit to me. I wouldn't do it. If I ever find a woman I'm going to marry, I won't fuck anybody else, ever. But I've never found a bird who could make me think that. Simple. **1998**

We've had the police after us for years. I dunno why they bother. They seem to have this idea that we're all huge dealers, which is stupid. Even if I wanted to be, which I don't, I'd be an idiot to get involved in drug dealing now with the band just getting our international prestige. **1982**

Normal life just isn't me. I don't agree with any politician. I thing they're all cunts. Tony fucking smiley Blair, he's just the same cunt as the last cunt. His suit's different. That's all. **1998**

Every time I go in and out of Britain to America I have to deal with that bullshit. They never stopped moaning about me being busted on New Years Eve 1972 for two fucking Mandrax, it's still on their file! I still get pulled over by customs 'cos I'm a dangerous homicidal maniac with drugs in my pocket for the schoolkids! **1996**

Listen, I don't think that any heavy metal band gets the credit they deserve. Iron Maiden go straight into the charts at Number 1 and they won't play it on Radio 1. I think that's fucking disgusting. What kind of a system is that? Whether they like it or not is immaterial, they play everything else and they should play the record That's selling the most in that particular week. It's disgraceful. It's one of the reasons that I moved to Los Angeles. **1991**

If you put a sticker on a record you're just encouraging a kid to buy it. He wants to know what's so wrong about it, so he'll buy it immediately against the wishes of his parents where before he might

have obeyed them. And now you're making the kid disobey their parents and isn't that smart. I just don't see the point of it. Censorship is always a loser. It wouldn't even work in Nazi Germany or Communist Russia, right?
1996

People in the bands are just practising all their adolescent lives, trying to get out there and play and then they get sucked in by these bastards. And you're surrounded suddenly by this group of backslappers. I hate them people! They are as far from me as politicians are. I have no time for them. Jesus! I execrate them. They are disgusting people!
1995

Blair's Britain seems to be just as horrible as the Conservative version, to me. I remember when Thatcher was in, I said "You're gonna miss that woman one day." She was a tyrant, but at least she was an English tyrant. And the two after her have seemed to be intent on selling bits of England to everybody who bids. They should give all the power back to the Royal Family. Divine right. Off with their 'ead. At least it would be more interesting. Public executions. It would be fun! **2000**

The PMRC never jumped on us because I don't sing about the devil so I don't have any problems with them. **1996**

I'm cleverer than the people who make assumptions about me. I'm smarter than they are 'cos I don't make assumptions. **1991**

I've never been a partisan of living in the country you were born in, that's just uninventive, really. To go and live somewhere else is a real turnaround, it makes you think of everything differently. Travel is the only real education, and it's the only way to find out about the other people in the world, because when you travel you see people as they really are. You're much more sympathetic to people for a start, you're a lot less prone to slogans like 'Kill The Argies', you know. We were in Argentina when they were doing all that in the papers, and it was arrant bullshit and lies. **2000**

I don't think about Tony Blair much. All I know is that he's reneged on every election promise he made so far. He's a piece of shit. Anyone who smiles that much has got to be untrustworthy. **2000**

We had this dressing room in Finland, which was a little caravan thing, and it had no booze in it so it didn't endear itself to us, you know. Kris Needs was walking around with a tree for some reason, and he put the tree through the window and broke it. It wasn't looking that great, and we were by a lake, so we thought we'd give it a Viking funeral. We set fire to it and pushed it out on the lake, and it looked really great, you know, it was dusk. It meandered out onto the lake and sank just as the sun went down. Then, of course, we got on the bus going back to the airport and the driver made the terrible mistake of saying, "You will not make a mess on my bus." Immediate food fight, with us down behind the seats throwing eggs at each other. His bus was in a bit of a state by the time we got to the airport, but you know, people shouldn't say these things to rock'n'roll bands, especially then. Now, of course, people would probably sit down and not do anything.

We were a real rock'n'roll band, it was us and Dr. Feelgood, which was fatal. When we got to customs, the official said, "Step into this room please." They didn't get Dr Feelgood for some reason, just Motörhead, and we were in there for three days. All we had between us was one copy of the *Melody Maker*, and I read that fucker, believe me, I read the adverts, the date at the bottom of the page, they finally deported us, and the funny thing was, we got on this plane and the captain came storming back to us and said, "I've heard about you. You guys are a disgrace to society! If you do anything on my plane, I'll have the police waiting for you at Heathrow", and all this. So we said, "Oh fuck, all right."

Of course, when we took off and got the drinks in, the first thing Eddie Clarke did in his exuberance was pour a vodka and orange down the neck of the woman in front of him. We didn't think that was too bad, though, but as soon as we got to Heathrow we saw all these police lined up on the tarmac! We thought, "Oh no, we're fucked here." But then they arrested the captain, he was drunk! Talk about poetic irony. **2000**

We've never had a good world, we don't understand how to make it a good world. The only thing we've learned in 2,000 years of civilisation is how to kill more people from further away, so we don't have to see it. Our mindset hasn't improved at all. **2000**

What can fans do to help combat censorship? Buy everything with a sticker on it immediately, possibly two copies. **1996**

Growing Old

I thought we had three years in us, if we were lucky. You don't think chronologically at the start, you only realise how long you've been around at the end. **2000**

I didn't know when it was gonna end. You open the door and every cat comes in. I just didn't wanna make too big a thing of the anniversary. We'd rather be considered contenders for what we're doing now, not some cabaret act. **2000**

I have become an icon. But I think it's fair, I do think it's fair. There are some people who you meet, and if they weren't there it would be necessary to invent them, I'm one of them. You guys need me, cause I'm that old cunt you can always come back to for a few choice epithets! It's true though, isn't it? I've been around a long time, and I remember back to Little Richard when he first came out, so you can always get a few quotes about that. Whatever you want to talk about in rock'n'roll, I've seen it. I can always dress up a bit.
It's fair, you need icons so you've got someone to talk about, you can't make an icon out of Bono, cause he knows fuck all. I mean the geezer said he liked Motörhead, thank you very much, but he knows fuck all. They're playing at it aren't they? **1989**

Oh, people slag me off. I answered a question on our website the other day from a guy who said, "Why don't Motörhead get out of the way and make room for some younger people?" and I said, "Because the young people aren't any fucking better, that's why." **2000**

Don't be ashamed of your music or your personal behaviour. You shouldn't do either. Just do the right thing. Everybody knows wrong from right. **1996**

I won't be a big musical force in the 21st Century. It's going to be very difficult chronologically-wise. People don't take much notice of us now as a musical direction. I think it's going to be very interesting and I'm probably glad I'm not going to see most of it. **1996**

You waste a lot of time sleeping, and people can catch up with you, see. When you sleep you become prey. I'd much rather be predator.
Sept 2000

I don't really want to be rich. You can't get a smile out of rich people with a fuckin' crowbar. They're usually miserable bastards they are. I knew a lot of millionaires in London from the Embassy Club. They're all miserable as shit. **1996**

It takes longer to get up in the morning. Apart from that, no, nothing has changed. There is still plenty of injustice to write about. Perhaps there is even more now. Perhaps I just know more about it now. **1996**

When they're 17, kids don't want to be like their parents, which is why my generation gave birth to all these accountants. **1999**

I get people coming up to me in LA going, "Hey, my main man, Lemmy! 'Ace Of Spades', dude!" I say, "You're not old enough to fucking remember it… you must have been about three when it came out. What are you talking about?" and they go, "Oh well, man, it was part of my formative years." Yeah, three years old. What did you do, stop shitting your pants or something? **1999**

People who expect to be happy fill me with dread. Happy is not a state to which you should aspire. You're going to be disappointed. **1996**

Jogging affects you worse than the fucking disease it's supposed to cure! People dropping like flies all over the fucking place on one-in-seven gradients, with big red faces, dying. It's great isn't it? Doggedly not smoking then sitting on the pavement outside the Cafe Barfly, about two feet from the traffic. How smart is that? **1999**

You can snatch bits of happiness but most of it is drudgery. Life has not been worked out very well with the powers that be. We're still at work and there's no reason for us to be there. Yeah, it's done with mirrors. I feel good about myself, and I know that I'm doing better than I was doing five or ten years ago. **1996**

You get a bit more impatient a bit quicker as time goes by. I liked my life 10 or 15 years ago, and I don't see why I should change it, if I like it. I just lived my life how I lived it, and people can like it or lump it, you know? It's always that way if you want to be an individual. I was always like that. That's why I kept getting fired out of all the other bands I was in. I had to form me own band to stop getting fired. **1999**

I don't mind the nostalgic element, so long as the new stuff gets listened to as well - that's all I ask. We're still making good music, you know? **2000**

When you look back you only see the good bits because your brain blacks out the bad bits to give you a break. I'm sure we've all fucked up every year of our lives and had a good time every year of our lives, you know? I'm not into looking at pinnacles, I like to look at the life as a life. And I've done pretty lucky, and I'm happy with that. Anyway, you shouldn't look for perfect. If you get 'very good'; you should be on your knees thanking somebody. **1999**

The most important thing in my life right now is trying to remember the chords to the bloody songs we just recorded for the album. **1996**

Ambitions? Yeah to fuck Raquel Welch, I hear she's pretty good. And I'd like to have another hit album before we go. The trouble is that the scene has deteriorated so drastically that people don't even listen to albums anymore, they just watch videos. Which is a terrible shame. **2000**

We stopped at the Rock 'n' Roll Hall Of Fame recently. It's in Cleveland and Cleveland has nothing to do with fucking rock'n'roll. It is the most un-rock'n'roll place I ever been in. That place is a joke, man. You walk into it and you have a TV showing clips and on each side of it you have a speaker with each one playing a different song – I mean you can't listen to either one. You just say "What is that?!" Then you have these stupid displays and a souvenir shop upstairs. It's just a joke. **1998**

Remember to always feel as beautiful as I look and to look as great as I feel. **1998**

There's bound to be a backlash sometime, we've had more than our share of good publicity. That's all right, it's juts part of the deal, innit? I regard it as inevitable. **1982**

I don't like fruit. It's too healthy. I don't recommend my lifestyle particularly. It worked for me, but it didn't for most of my friends. **1995**

You don't have to be afraid, you don't have to listen to anybody. You have to keep yourself pure - and I don't mean wear a condom. Impure has nothing to do with shit like that. Mankind invented the word "guilt", and it was attached to religion. You do not need to be guilty, you do not need to be put down. Your soul is your own and you know right from wrong. Everybody does. If they didn't, they wouldn't do the wrong things at night and hide them. Everybody knows what the wrong shit is - don't do it. Be honourable and don't die ashamed of anything. Treat people as you would be treated yourself. That's my fucking story right there. **1995**

I've been in movies and it was boring. Show up at 5.30am, have a roll and coffee and sit there all day in the company of bloody actors. **2000**

You know, I'm running out of time here. I'm 54, what the fuck am I doing wasting a day like this? **2000**

When we fly, I like to think I'm a World War Two pilot, you know, we're coming down with a wing on fire and only one wheel left. I know that once you're past the age of 30 you're not supposed to think like that, but I don't give a damn. After 30 you're supposed to settle down with one and a half kids, polish the car on Sunday and finish in time for lunch. Well that's all bullshit as far as I'm concerned. That's a living death. It's not worth a toss. **1984**

Die You Bastard?

After I die, there'll be no Motörhead because you couldn't get a singer to do this or play bass like that. You probably could but it wouldn't really work. Mikkey Dee (the current drummer) is like that. Phil Campbell is almost there too. People that you just can't replace. I'll continue until I drop fuckin' dead. **1996**

I think if your number's up, your number's up. Might as well be fatalistic about it. People could throw a can on stage and it could kill you. If you worried about that it would drive you crazy. **1982**

The occasional bout of flu might lay me up for a couple of days, but I always believe that if you lie down germs have more chance of attacking you; keep moving and it confuses them. **1979**

The thing is, why would I pack it in? Because I'm good at what I do, and we fill a niche that would be unfilled forever if we went, because there's nobody like us. And you deserve us, anyway. **2000**

I don't even consider suicide as an option you know. I never thought of that and I got a sense of humour, which a lot of people don't know. A lot of time when chicks get old they feel they're not wanted and are not appealing anymore. With guys you can get old and still feel good. **1998**

Lets hope that I fall with some grace. I'll probably land on some ugly tattooed woman. 1996 What keeps us going? Just dogged persistence. A refusal to lie down and play dead. If we break up and give, then a lot of people that I don't like were right. I won't fucking give it to them. A lot of people I do like would be right as well, and I wouldn't give it to them either. **1998**

It would be a good place to die, on stage. Well, what's the alternative? Die in bed sick and old? **1996**

I don't want to live "forever", it's a long time. You could be 294 and not reach "forever". but I think you'd be sick of it by then. I think anybody would be sick of it by then. Even me. And I like to stay up late, you know? Actually, I'd like to die the year before forever. To avoid the rush. **1999**

Dave Grohl (top) and
Joey Ramone.

Ace Geezer
(Testimonials from others)

He was, and still remains, one of the all time great rock'n'roll characters. But he was a handful, to say the least. **Dave Brock, 1999**

Lemmy is a true rock legend, and he's still fronting the loudest, most exciting live metal-core punk band around, a band who put others half their age to complete and utter shame. In short, Motörhead will blow your mind, rupture your appendix and let you experience rock'n'roll just the way it was always meant to be.
Joey Ramone, 2000

Lemmy is truly the king of rock'n'roll to me, always has been, always will be. Fuck Elvis. **Dave Grohl, 2000**

I've always hit the drums pretty hard, and Lemmy has the reputation of being loud – because he's partly deaf. **Phil Taylor, 1978**

Nothing can kill him. No disease could live in his body.
Howard Benson (*Bastards* LP producer), 1995

I met Lemmy through speed really. Y'know, dealing and scoring. I wasn't actually playing in a band at the time. **Phil Taylor, 2000**

You hear a lot of good things and a lot of bad things about Lemmy, and most of them are true. He is a cunt,

he is a bastard, he does knock other people's chicks off. But he's also incredibly funny. Every time you go out with him it's a memorable experience.
Phil Taylor

We had a bond, and it went beyond whether you liked someone or not. Me and Phil were especially close because Lemmy was a bit of a loner. I can't image being any closer to anyone else than those two, and it never even entered my mind whether I even liked Lemmy or not, because it wasn't even an issue. We felt almost indestructible because we'd had so much shit thrown at us and we'd decided that no matter what happened, we were gonna fuckin' carry on.
Eddie Clarke, 2000

Lemmy is way ahead of anyone else. People like yourself pick up on it now, but it has been a slow progress. Lemmy has been writing great lyrics for years, and nobody has said a word about them.
Phil Taylor, 1995

I saw Hawkwind for the first time when I was 12 years old. It was right after Space Ritual Live and it changed my life. I have seen them four times all together. I still have Lemmy's autograph. He's the only one that came out. He was probably looking for chicks. **Phil Taylor, 1995**

Motörhead will beep on as they are till one of us drops dead. Obviously Lemmy's the prime candidate being 35... **Phil Taylor, 1982**

He was a great innovator - he played his bass like a rhythm guitar... and his charismatic impact was immense. The way Hawkwind sacked him was utterly foolish and quite unforgivable... the worst thing that happened in the entire history of the band. They lost a very important part of their character, and a lot of their driving force. They also lost a loyal guy... Lemmy has his faults, but changing his tune is not one of them! **Robert Calvert**

One of the few songs we'd finished was called 'Bomber', so that became the title. It was all very rush, rush. but Lemmy always had great titles - things that just got your imagination working like mad. **Eddie Clarke, 2000**

Lemmy is a fucking masterpiece really the way he works. He works so fucking hard. He never stops really except when he falls over and has to have a rest! He is getting on now, he is well into his fifties and he hasn't had a break! I am fucked and I *have* had a break! He has just carried on. **Fast Eddie Clarke, 2000**

In the days when he used to sell speed, you could guarantee if he sold you a gram it was probably half a gram. He's very good at making you feel guilty. He's definitely got the gift of the gab on his side. **Phil Taylor 1979**

He is still going and he is still lucid. It is not like talking to a plank of wood or anything – he is still all there so it is fucking nice. Whenever I see him I always get a nice warm feeling to see that he is okay because the thing that we had between us, me, Phil and him was so special. You realise later just how special it was and that it really only happens once in your life, that sort of camaraderie where it is you against the world and you haven't got any money and you are fighting everybody but you are doing it together.
As long as the band is OK you have got something. You have a few fans in the beginning and then they grow and become an army and in the end you have to say, "Well, yeah, Motörhead are here" because we just were not going to go away. **Eddie Clarke 2000**

If you have got a big fat bass there you can kind of lose your guitar a bit. It takes the edge off of it and makes it sort of nice and warm but when you are playing with Lemmy and the drummer it just sort of makes it really hard and cutting so you can't really relax with the Motörhead sound. You are forever having to keep your eye on it and hold it down as it were. I mean, the drugs might have had something to do with that, I'm not sure!
Eddie Clarke 2000

The only things that really mattered to us was the partying and the music and it is still really the same but Lemmy is the only one with a band to do it in!
Eddie Clarke 2000

We don't serve punk rockers here.
Staff at the Man in the Moon pub, Kings Road, Chelsea in 1978 while ejecting Lemmy & co

Motörhead and Girlschool: 'Fast' Eddie, Kim, Phil, Enid, Denise, Lemmy and Kelly .